Holding on to the Land and the Lord

Holding on to the Land and the Lord

Kinship, Ritual, Land Tenure, and Social Policy in the Rural South

ROBERT L. HALL AND CAROL B. STACK, EDITORS

Southern Anthropological Society Proceedings, No. 15
Robert L. Blakely, Series Editor

The University of Georgia Press
Athens, Georgia 30602

Southern Anthropological Society

Founded 1966

OFFICERS 1980–1981

Mary W. Helms, President
Elizabeth M. Eddy, President-Elect
David M. Johnson, Secretary-Treasurer
Alice Murphree, Councilor
Louise M. Robbins, Councilor
Solon T. Kimball, Councilor
Robert L. Blakely, Series Editor
Nancy H. Owen, Newsletter Editor

Program Coordinator, 1981:
Andrew W. Miracle, Jr.

Copyright © 1982 by the Southern Anthropological Society
All rights reserved

Set in 10 on 12 point Times Roman type
Printed in the United States of America

Library of Congress Cataloging in Publication Data

Holding on to the land and the Lord.

(Southern Anthropological Society proceedings; no. 15)
Essays originally presented at the 15th annual meeting of the Southern
Anthropological Society, held in Louisville, Ky., March 21, 1980.

Includes bibliographical references.
1. Southern States—Rural conditions—Addresses, essays, lectures. 2. Kin-
ship—Southern States—Addresses, essays, lectures. 3. Christianity—Southern
States—Addresses, essays, lectures. 4. Land tenure—Southern States—Ad-
dresses, essays, lectures. I. Hall, Robert L. II. Stack, Carol B. III. Southern
Anthropological Society. IV. Series.
GN2.S9243 no. 15 [HN79.A13]   301s   81-12926
ISBN 0-8203-0584-7   [307.7'2'0975]   AACR2
ISBN 0-8203-0596-0 (pbk.)

Contents

Preface
Robert L. Hall and Carol B. Stack   vii

Introduction
Robert L. Hall and Carol B. Stack   3

PART ONE: KINSHIP IN A POLITICAL CONTEXT

Kinship in a Changing Economy: A View from the Sea Islands
Kay Young Day   11

The Contradictions of a Kinship Community
Allen Batteau   25

Black Leadership Patterns and Political Change in the American South
Yvonne V. Jones   41

Fortress without Walls: A Black Community after Slavery
Sydney Nathans   55

PART TWO: THE DYNAMICS OF RITUAL AND CONVERSION

The Conversion Ritual in a Rural Black Baptist Church
Charles Williams   69

The Role of Aesthetics in the Conversion Experience in a Missionary
Baptist Church
John A. Forrest   80

The Religious Interpretation of Experience in a Rural Black Community
Bruce T. Grindal   89

Language, Vision, Myth: The Primitive Baptist Experience of Grace
Brett Sutton   102

Comments on Part Two
James L. Peacock   115

PART THREE: LAND TENURE AND SOCIAL POLICIES

Peasants and Policy: Comparative Perspectives on Aging
B. Lisa Gröger   121

The Last of the Tenant Farmers in the Old New South:
A Case Study of Tenancy in Franklin County, North Carolina
Steven Petrow   131

Appalachian Families, Landownership, and Public Policy
Patricia D. Beaver   146

The Contributors   155

Index   159

Preface

These essays present the results of fieldwork conducted in the southern United States by anthropologists and historians in various stages of their career development. Our contributors range from graduate students to seasoned professionals who have already made significant contributions to the scholarly literature.

The eleven essays gathered in this volume were originally prepared for presentation at the Key Symposium of the fifteenth annual meeting of the Southern Anthropological Society held in Louisville, Kentucky, on March 21, 1980. The general topic of the symposium, "The Rural South, Problems and Prospects," was subdivided into a morning session entitled "Complexities of Change" and an afternoon session "The Religious Experience." The papers from both sessions were shuffled, paired, dissected, and reassembled in a number of experimental groupings before we reached the final configuration of three parts that appears here.

The task of molding these independently written essays into a coherent collection has proved to be difficult and challenging. We also found that we had to make agonizing choices about revisions and which papers to include. No such task is ever easy. One of the most rewarding outcomes of putting together this volume was the broadening of vision experienced by the editors. Each of us was at least momentarily liberated from the tunnel vision that too often derives from immersion in one's discipline or specialty. We have come to a significantly greater appreciation of the extent to which kinship, religion, and land tenure are linked to each other and embedded in larger political and economic processes.

Although we received encouragement and support from a number of people, several deserve special mention. All of the essays were revised in light of the fine comments and suggestions made by the discussants. Conrad Arensberg and Molly Dougherty commented on the "Complexities of Change" and Solon Kimball and Robert Hall were discussants for the papers on "The Religious Experience." Each of the papers, and this volume in its entirety, has benefited greatly from their thoughtful contributions. James Peacock provided inspiration for this volume both as a teacher and scholar, and as the behind-the-scenes organizer for the afternoon session. His introductory remarks to that session are included in Part Two. Thanks also go to Sydney Nathans, whose admonitions inspired us to clarify our thoughts. Bob Blakely has provided constant though gentle grousing. To his credit and style, this volume is complete. We wish to thank Connie Rayborn, the administrative assistant for the Center for the Study of the Family and the State at Duke University, who organized the administrative details, communication, and typing throughout the year, during her vacation, and during the last several weekends of the project. She is wonderful. Only in rare instances are indexers acknowledged, however we are extremely grateful to Deborah Shaw. She has provided an index that will be a useful and accurate guide for a variety of readers who may enjoy this collection.

Robert L. Hall
Carol B. Stack

Holding on to the Land and the Lord

Introduction

ROBERT L. HALL AND CAROL B. STACK

Even today, scholars and the general public tend to think of rural communities as isolated, relatively self-contained entities in which essentially cooperative and communal values may be preserved intact. Clearly, the rural communities discussed in these essays have traditional values to protect. Enormous value is placed on land and landownership, kin loyalty and cooperation, and on church membership. Yet the essays in this volume also make clear that these values are all caught in a turbulence emanating from the external world. The divided and competitive industrial economy has found its way into the daily lives of these rural southern communities, however isolated they were or sought to be.

The four papers in Part One, "Kinship in a Political Context," share a focus on the functioning of kin networks and the politics of kinship in several different geographical and ethnic contexts within the rural South. In the first paper, Kay Day examines the kin networks of the Mt. Pleasant black community in the Sea Islands of South Carolina, and finds them to be a resource providing resistance to the pressures toward economic ranking exerted by the larger society. Day's analysis provides a singular focus on the harmonious, supportive, and cooperative aspects of kinship—a refuge and a resource in a largely externally controlled world. In her discussion of Day's paper, Molly Dougherty highlighted the fact that on the South Carolina coast, "it is kinship, principally mutual aid and a sense of separate identity, that promotes continuity in the face of widespread social change."

Allan Batteau's study of a mountain community in Kentucky provides a counterpoint to Day's emphasis on the positive, nonconflictive elements of kinship. Contradictions and conflicts are masked beneath the ideology of "we are all kin." It should not be surprising that the actual behaviors in this mountain community often contradict the ideology of intense neighborhood and kin solidarity. The creative tension between rhetoric and reality, between verbalizations about behavior and actual behavior, is one of the most pervasive universals in human society, one which has long been the meaty stuff of anthropological and historical inquiry. Furthermore, Batteau's own discomfort with the "troubling" and seemingly contradictory data about the factional nature of kinship derives precisely from one of these rhetoric/reality dichotomies: "the professional rhetoric" that requires anthropologists to label certain kin relationships a "kinship system" may obscure their focus on the way informants themselves actually think about family relations and kin ties. As Dougherty indicated in her comments, formal kinship analysis does not always show the way kin relations really work on a day-to-day basis. Instead, Dougherty suggests kinship operates "more like a network, where fluidity in group identity permits local factions to petition the powerful." Sometimes, by assuming that there is such a thing as a unitary kinship system, anthropologists overlook such discrete, but sometimes overlapping, domains or functions of community living as social class, personal identity, householding, and child-raising. Perhaps the most "troubling data" of all, and a thread that runs throughout the papers in this volume, is the existence of great inequalities of wealth in these and other rural areas, and the politics of kinship in this context. As Batteau himself writes, "The basic datum for understanding these contradictions is the stratification of the community."

Yvonne Jones's study of patterns of black leadership in a rural Piedmont, North Carolina, county examines the impact of recent changes in the jural status of black Americans on local politics. After describing the strategies and techniques utilized by blacks to exert influence during the era of black disenfranchisement (from the late 1890s to the mid-1960s), Jones identifies shifts in ethnic boundaries that have occurred since the 1960s. Finally, she shows the influence of these boundary changes on the traditional white system of patronage. As Dougherty observed in her discussion, "Jones provides a useful typology of the roles of brokers and entrepreneurs and demonstrates their functions in maintaining communication and facilitating change . . . where political action is used to improve the economic circumstances of residents."

Sydney Nathans distills the story of three generations in the history of a black community that began in the 1840s when 109 slaves were forced to migrate from their home in North Carolina to a newly opened cotton plantation in Alabama. His study provides unusual historical depth to our understanding of black immigrants in slavery and freedom. He depicts a community that has maintained remarkable continuity over time and explores the mechanisms—kinship, land-holding, religion—by which each generation "held on to the land and the Lord." His paper serves as a natural bridge from the study of southern kinship to the exploration of southern religion.

In the four papers in Part Two, "The Dynamics of Ritual and Conversion," patterns of kinship, mutual aid, and land tenure, all hallmarks of the rural South, recede into the background as the focus shifts to Protestant religious ritual and symbolic patterns that occur within those contexts. The papers contain lively accounts of field observations in the upper South and in the deep South. All focus on the ritual forms associated with the conversion experience. Charles Williams's description of six stages in the conversion ritual in a rural black Baptist church in Mississippi is based primarily on his own involvement in that church. Such a strategy entails dilemmas: how one may report the contents of extensive fieldwork conducted in one's own home church and natal community without violating the privacy of unique religious conversion experiences or the canons of balanced scholarship, whether the anthropologist can become ethnographically aware of his own life experiences to the point that he can be both reporter and actor in certain kinds of ethnographic situations. By himself Williams is an ethnographic informant.

John Forrest addresses a theoretical question in aesthetics using ethnographic materials from a congregation of white Missionary Baptists in the swamplands of North Carolina. He argues not only that this congregation constitutes an aesthetic community which shares criteria for aesthetic judgments, but also that members of this community manipulate the physical and ritual forms with the intention of provoking desired behavior—namely the conversion of new members to the church. Forrest's suggestion that the spatial arrangement of congregation, aisles, choir, and pulpit somehow reflects theological and behavioral expectations needs to be more widely tested in comparative ethnographic research among southern Protestant denominations.

In his study of the religious interpretations of experience in ten churches in a black community in rural north Florida, Bruce Grindal argues that a large number of individuals in this community experience spontaneous and intensely personal dramatic encounters with God that they later talk about in communal settings. Oral narratives about these visionary experiences become integral parts of public worship services to varying degrees.

Brett Sutton's paper focuses on narratives of grace, particularly the accounts of visions in a black Primitive Baptist church in North Carolina's Piedmont area. Emphasizing their predestinarian theology rather than their ethnicity, Sutton finds the visionary narratives to be unusually stable forms among both black and white Primitive Baptists. The style and imagery of the vision narratives collected and analyzed by Sutton do not seem to be peculiar to the Primitive Baptists. Yet he may be correct that the formal, predictable use of personal vision narratives in public worship may be more prevalent among Primitive Baptists.

An unresolved problem emerges from an examination of the four papers in Part Two: what is the relationship between the degree of ritual ecstasy and social stratification? The authors found varying degrees of spontaneity and emotional ecstasy both within and across denominations, within and across ethnic groupings. Grindal and Williams suggest that Afro-American ethnicity imposes a shared quality to the religious behavior of black Americans regardless of denominational affiliation. This widely perceived commonality within the ethnic group has led a number of writers to postulate that there is such a thing as "black religion" or "black religiosity." Two of the most striking and persistent behaviors which leave an impression of Afro-American cultural distinctiveness are shouting and the religious dance. The uniqueness of such behaviors is, we contend, as much shadow as substance, as much an artifact of racial, regional, and class modes of perception as externally verifiable social fact. The cultural fact of the matter is that some whites, reds, and others in the South have been known to engage in almost all the religious activities which are widely thought to be uniquely or distinctively black religious behaviors: glossalalia, vision testimonies, religious dancing, lining out hymns, ecstatic prayer and preaching, baptism by immersion, and footwashing. The dozens of descriptions of "strange" southern black religious behavior written by nineteenth-century Congregationalist missionaries and by northern Unitarians like Henry George Spaulding tend to convince one that the perceived strangeness of the events described derives as much from differences in denominational affiliation, regional origin, and class standing as from any rigid black/white cultural dichotomy. The underlying analytical problem raised by the four papers in Part Two, taken together, is how to explain the baffling and colorful array of orders of service, musical styles, oratory, personal narratives, and even spatial arrangements found in the religious activities of blacks, whites, and others living in the rural South.

The three papers in Part Three, "Land Tenure and Social Policies," describe land tenure, stratification, and the impact of social policies on lifeways in various rural areas in the South. Lisa Gröger begins her analysis with a comparison of the French and American commitments to the small family farm and the consequences of particular policy measures. In her paper both the categories of farms and of individuals reflect the life cycle and class structure of an agrarian-based North Carolina community. In an analysis of preliminary data from this study of small tobacco farmers in the Piedmont region of North Carolina, Gröger explores the politics and rationale of tobacco allotments in the United States and the impact of these allotments on the small family farmer, particularly the aging family farmer. The paper shows how tobacco farmers are forced to support policies that are in the interests of large tobacco companies, policies that have resulted from large-scale and well-financed lobbying efforts by a multitude of groups with conflicting interests. In this system the small farmer dependent on tobacco assumes the risk and the burden of crop failure, while the tobacco companies do not have to get deeply involved in production themselves. A frequent theme in southern rural communities, as Dougherty mentioned in her comments, is that "unexpected and undesired consequences of policy formulated beyond the local community seem to be an unfortunate inevitability."

Steven Petrow describes the elaborate system of tenancy in an intensive case study of tenancy in a single North Carolina county. He delineates the three basic types of tenant farming (cash tenancy, cash-share farming, and sharecropping), the hierarchy of white and black tenant farmers, and the demise of the tenant farm population. Petrow further examines the element of risk as it pertains to the relationship between landlord and tenant. The landlord and tenant are expected to share equally the risk of a failed or diseased crop despite the enormous burden this places on the typical sharecropper.

Taken together, the papers by Gröger and Petrow explore the politics and ecology of land tenure and tobacco allotments in the Piedmont region of North Carolina. Gröger examines the ecology of land tenure from the point of view of the small landowning farmer to whom the tobacco allotment is a major productive resource. Petrow, on another hand, emphasizes the point of view of the landless tenant farmer.

Given the economic situation of most small farmers and subsistence agriculturalists in the rural South, industrial and technological development is indeed a mixed blessing. Furniture and textile industries, and other low-wage industries, for the most part offer seasonal or dead-end jobs. Yet landownership and the industrial economy, farmers and nonfarm employment, are inextricably bound. This relationship is affected by and has influence on patterns of land tenure and the wage structure of industrial employment, especially in the rural South. Gröger, Beaver, and Petrow describe landowners who in differing degrees would be on the margin of survival if they had only their land and its crops as the basis of survival. Yet the industrial employment available to farm inhabitants is no less precarious. What evolves is a portrait of families whose livelihoods are marginal both as farmers and as industrial workers. They are an integral part of one system composed of farming and industry. Without low-paying off-farm wages they would be forced to abandon the land, and without the land they would be unable to survive without federal assistance.

Patricia Beaver's treatment of Appalachian families and landownership provides a link between discussions contained elsewhere in this volume on landownership, kinship, cultural resources, and economic development. She sees the mountain family falling through the cracks, unable to maintain a land base and yet structurally excluded from jobs that provide good salaries and opportunities for upward mobility. This is exacerbated by land speculation, recreational development, federal landownership, and landownership restrictions which, until recently, were barriers to receiving federal assistance. Beaver's conclusion, that public policy in the United States is essentially urban policy, should serve us not only as a keen observation on the past, but as a guideline for research and advocacy in the future.

Part One
Kinship in a Political Context

Kinship in a Changing Economy: A View from the Sea Islands

KAY YOUNG DAY

The blacks of Mt. Pleasant, a Sea Island community on the coast of South Carolina, have a unique history as a landowning peasantry (Rose 1964; Woofter 1930). Their peasant mode of production persisted alongside the plantation system until capitalist expansion and industrial development displaced black farmers following World War II. Even as their productive activities shifted from the farm to wage labor in recent decades, the blacks of Mt. Pleasant have held onto their lands and their communities. They have maintained their traditional way of life despite economic changes that forced millions of blacks and whites elsewhere in the South off the land and into the cities.

Mt. Pleasant lies just across the Cooper River from Charleston. The town of Mt. Pleasant looks much like any other metropolitan suburb; shopping centers, fast food chains, and tract houses dominate the landscape for miles. This suburban growth has occurred in the last twenty-five years, much of it within the last ten years. Since World War II, the white population has grown considerably in Mt. Pleasant and Charleston, an area that was overwhelmingly black for most of South Carolina's history. Beyond the town limits of Mt. Pleasant, the countryside looks much as it did a century ago. Large tracts of uninhabited land were the sites of plantations until recently. Interspersed among these tracts are densely populated black communities, numbering 300 to 500 inhabitants each. There are eight black communities in the unincorporated area of Mt. Pleasant. Each community is geographically distinct and bears a name by which its inhabitants are identified. These communities are closely linked to one another through ties of kinship and marriage that have developed over the generations.

The black communities of Mt. Pleasant were created by freed men and women who obtained land in the 1870s and 1880s. The inhabitants of these communities today are the descendants of the original community founders. The clusters of family compounds in each community—Horlbeck Corner, Johnson Hill, Jackson Town and so on—bear the names of these founding ancestors. These family compounds, ranging from three to twenty households, are the centers of domestic activities: women congregate in the yard to keep company while weaving baskets and minding children; men and boys gather to work on someone's car, to clean the day's catch of fish, or to make house repairs; there is a constant scurry of children from house to house; and, without asking, it is hard to tell to whom the children belong or where they live. Beyond the family compounds are congregating spots of community social life: the "juke" where men relax after the workday, and where both men and women socialize on weekends; the sports field where community teams play against each other every week; the society halls where members hold their monthly meetings and sponsor fund-raising events; and the Praise House where community members gather weekly for the support and fellowship of religious ritual.

This essay examines how kin and community organization, created as part of an earlier peasant farming tradition, have sustained Mt. Pleasant blacks in their transition from an agrarian to an industrial society. In particular, this essay focuses on the role of kin and family in pursuing economic activities—in making a living, in gaining access to resources, and in securing support for coping with white-dominated economic institutions. The recent development of industrial capitalism in the South offers an uncommon opportunity to examine the changes accompanying this process among people who retain strong ties to the past and to a particular place. Moreover, in Mt. Pleasant it is possible to document these changes in the lives and memories of people whose bonds of kin, community, and family span well over a century.

The older generation of Mt. Pleasant blacks grew up on family farms of from ten to fifty acres. These farming families grew most of what they ate. Rice, corn, sweet potatoes, millet, a variety of summer vegetables, and a few domestic animals provided the bulk of the family diet. Their diet was supplemented by fish, shrimp, crab, and oysters gathered from tidal estuaries that lace the coastal mainland. The silt-rich black soil and the abundant marine life yielded ample sustenance for the family's needs.

Self-sufficiency in food production among the black farmers was based on a patrimony in land provided by their ancestors, "the Old People" as they are called. "The Old People" are revered as the generation who came through slavery, acquired land, and set about the arduous task of clearing land on which they established their homes, their farms, and their communities. These community founders obtained land from the plantations where they had resided as slaves. After emancipation, freed men and women gained title to fifteen- or twenty-acre plots of land in return for stipulated amounts of labor on the plantation, usually two or three days a week for three years. The practice of selling land to blacks was a concession that many Sea Island planters made in order to maintain a labor force (Murray 1949; Williamson 1965).

Landownership provided Mt. Pleasant blacks a means of independence from the plantation and from the sharecropping, tenancy, and lien systems that bound blacks and whites elsewhere in the South in a cycle of indebtedness and control by landlords. Free from the dictates of landlords, the blacks of Mt. Pleasant managed their farms according to the needs of the family (Bethel 1981). With the exception of a few large farms, half the land or more was cultivated in food crops while a smaller portion was devoted to cotton, the mainstay of the agrarian cash economy until the 1930s and 1940s.

In addition to subsistence farming and cotton production, the people of Mt. Pleasant engaged in a wide range of entrepreneurial activities to supplement family income. The city of Charleston afforded an easily accessible market for a variety of goods: vegetables, seafood, baskets, fishing nets, flowers, beaver pelts, and so on. Marketing goods in Charleston was a comparatively lucrative business. It was not unusual for men and women to make fifteen or twenty dollars in one day's sale of vegetables or seafood. Mrs. Ada Habersham, who sold vegetables regularly in the Charleston municipal market during the 1920s and 1930s, states: "You could make some money [selling vegetables in the market] 'cause that used to be the only place for people to buy vegetables. Even the stores come right to us to get the things wholesale." Black farmers and fishermen were the main producers of foodstuffs for the city until World War II.

The family's income from farming, fishing, and marketing also was augmented by wage labor on the plantations and in the city of Charleston. Until recently, in fact, black workers constituted the vast majority of the labor force in Charleston (Tindall 1952). They even held skilled jobs as brick masons, carpenters, and artisans, and worked in local factories, much to the dismay of upstate businessmen, who reserved skilled labor and factory jobs for whites (ibid.). With the exception of some skilled labor jobs, wages were extremely low, since there was an abundant supply of black labor in the Charleston area. Until the 1930s these jobs were undertaken primarily on a seasonal or temporary basis to supplement the family's immediate cash needs. Among blacks in the more remote parts of the Sea Islands, temporary migration to Charleston or Savannah satisfied part of the family's cash needs (Kiser 1969).

For the families of Mt. Pleasant, securing a livelihood in the agrarian, nonindustrial economy required the labor of all members of the household. Children eight or nine years old assumed a portion of domestic tasks while teenagers and young adults engaged in farm work, fishing, and wage labor. Harold Adams, now in his seventies, performed many of these tasks in his youth during the 1920s and 1930s. He was the youngest member of a household consisting of his parents, six brothers and sisters, and his paternal grandmother. As a young boy his primary duty was caring for his grandmother, who had been a slave on a nearby plantation and lived to be 125 years old. Later in his youth Harold worked in the fields with his father. Once the fields were prepared and the crops planted, Harold and his father and brothers, along with other men in the community, spent most of the summer catching fish that they sold to a nearby island resort. During the winter, he worked either on local plantations or at the shipyard in Mt. Pleasant. Harold spent most of his early adulthood "working to help out the family." In 1930, he got a full-time job installing waterworks on a nearby island. As the youngest son, he assumed much of the responsibility for his aging parents and the children of his sisters who lived in Charleston. In 1945, at the age of 29, Harold married and established a household on his family's land.

Women were also active in the family's pursuit of a livelihood. Woofter, in his 1930 study of a Sea Island black community, noted repeatedly that the key to a farmer's success was an "energetic wife." Some couples even divided their land and competed with each other in farm operations. Other successful farm operations were run entirely by women, mostly widows. In Mt. Pleasant as well, women assumed an equal role in farming and often worked jointly with their husbands.

In many families, husbands and wives divided their work activities. In the Porcher family, for example, Charles devoted his labor to fishing while Maggie took on the primary responsibility for the family farm. Charles and his older sons were members of a black fishing cooperative, the "Mosquito Fleet," which supplied seafood to Charleston. Maggie maintained an active trade in marketing vegetables, flowers, and baskets which she produced with the help of her children and grandchildren, who also resided in the family compound. Because of the long growing season on the coast (300 days), Maggie was able to produce vegetables for almost the entire year.

Many women of Maggie's generation (50 years or older in 1930) continued their farming and marketing activities through the 1920s, 1930s, and 1940s, decades when the agrarian and urban economies were rapidly changing. In the 1920s and 1930s cotton production declined because of boll weevil infestation and changing agricultural markets. Truck farming began to replace cotton production along the coast. While some farmers who owned 50–100 acres attempted to engage in large-scale vegetable production for northern markets, most black farmers did not have the necessary capital or sufficient acreage to make this transition. Eventually, Mt. Pleasant blacks were displaced from local markets as well. As the service sector of the economy expanded after World War II to accommodate a growing urban population, shrimping trawlers and chain grocery stores took over the markets once dominated by blacks.

At the same time that blacks were displaced in their farming, fishing, and marketing activities, jobs were created in the postwar urban-industrial economy. With this development, however, occupations became clearly segregated along racial lines. Whites who migrated to Charleston found jobs in industry, while blacks were relegated to service jobs that paid little, left employees subject to underemployment, and held few possibilities for occupational mobility. In the wake of these changes of the last three decades, many residents of Mt. Pleasant joined other southern blacks migrating to northern cities in search of better wages, education, and skills. There are few families today who do not have kin living in distant cities. Others have remained in Mt. Pleasant despite obvious constraints. For those people who have stayed, and for those who have returned to Mt. Pleasant, the community remains the center of social life and the nexus of support, cooperation, and resources.

In the Mt. Pleasant black communities, social relations and rights to land and other resources are governed by kinship. Social organization in these communities is characterized by localized patrilineal descent groups and bilateral kindreds. Thus, both men and women have rights to land; it is usually men, however, who actually establish residences on "family land." The cultural ideal in Mt. Pleasant black communities is patrilocal residence: "The woman is supposed to go where the man at." The statistical reality in residence patterns reflects this patrilocal preference—73 percent of married couples reside on the husband's land.[1] Although women usually leave the family compound upon marriage, the close proximity of the communities into which they marry allows them to maintain close ties with their own family and kin.

The ties with one's descent group form the primary basis of identity within the community. A person is referred to as a Simmons, a Horlbeck, a Gaillard, et cetera. Being a member of a certain descent group identifies individuals with specific physical, linguistic, and behavioral attributes. Descent group affiliation also is the basis for ranking individuals according to economic and social standing in the community. For men, patrilineal affiliation is expressed in naming practices. Men are almost always named after their fathers and their fathers' kin, while women are named after kindred members and "godparents." This traditional way of naming males, incidentally, makes it possible to trace family lineages back generations in manuscript censuses and plantation inventories.

Although lineage membership is an important factor in community social relations and in gaining rights to certain resources and skills—particularly for men—the day-to-day cooperative units consist of smaller lineage segments and networks of kin. Those who share in the daily exchange of goods and services are referred to as "close family." "Close family" consists of parents, adult children and their children, and some collateral relatives on both the mother's and father's side. Other kin and nonkin may be recruited into this domestic network as well.

For the people of Mt. Pleasant, family is an important determinant of economic advantages and available options.[2] Families who have been able to manage their resources, and thereby provide family members with assets, are the most tightly knit and prestigious families in the community. These families are referred to as "big families of people." "Big" families are large because sons and daughters find it beneficial to maintain these ties. Their family compounds resemble small villages of fifteen to twenty-five households. The benefits of allegiance to particular families are often deciding factors in marriage choices and residence.

The primary economic asset that individuals inherit from their parents is land. Although land is no longer the means of livelihood today, rights to land are an important social and economic investment in a family estate. The availability of land and the aid of kin are the means of establishing a household independent of rent and indebtedness to whites and their financial institutions. Kin assist in house construction by providing labor, skills, and building materials, and sometimes through direct financial help. In cases where a family's land holdings are not sufficient to accommodate the needs of their children, parents seek additional land through appeals to kin on both sides of the family, or through purchase from local whites. Land is not a commodity that is sold, but a right that is transferred to kin as needed.

Rights to land and land use are controlled by the oldest members of the family. They hold the deeds to family property.[3] Upon the death of the eldest member, land is divided up among the children. Providing land for one's children and controlling land deeds and land use are important ways by which older people insure rights to their children's labor and secure for themselves care and support in old age (Bethel 1981). The connection between children's support and a patrimony in land was pointed out most clearly to me by an elderly woman who produces and markets baskets with the help of her daughters. As she was explaining to me the benefits of having children, she got up from her highway basket stand and led me to a clearing in the woods. From where we stood, her whole family compound was visible: "My land go all the way back to the wood there. You see that white stick there—well, that's where it stop. All the houses you see—those are my children's houses. . . . This land here is Miss Mary one [a white woman]. I think she might sell it. If she do, I want to get that for my children too."

This highly localized kin network, based on a family estate, provides mutual support and care for all its members—young and old. In earlier decades, elderly men and women were the heads of family productive units centered on farming, fishing, and marketing. Through their families, individuals also acquired skills in trades such as net-making, boat-building, basket-making, blacksmithing, bricklaying, and carpentry. As the younger generation of men and women have moved into the workplace, these traditional skills and patterns of cooperation have remained important in securing jobs and in organizing productive activities alternative to wage labor.

For men, the articulation of traditional skills with jobs created in the expanding industrial economy has been particularly advantageous, especially in the construction industry. In the 1930s and 1940s, when land development began, the construction industry had at its disposal a local population already trained in these skills. Sixty percent of the men in Mt. Pleasant today work in the construction industry.[4] The older men got these jobs either through previously acquired skills or by connections that their kinsmen had with white employers. Today, a new generation is gaining employment by the same means. For this reason, family groups tend to be occupational groups. In the Simmons family, for example, each of the three lineage segments represents an occupational concentration: plumbing, carpentry, and shrimping.

Skills are usually passed down from father to son. Within the larger context of kin, jobs and skills for men commonly follow patrilineal lines. Ike Simmons learned plumbing while working under his father, who was in charge of waterworks on a nearby island development. Upon his father's advice, Ike quit that job for a better-paying one which he secured through Nat, his father's brother's son. On this new job, Ike became a foreman, and was in a position to hire other men. He hired his brother and trained him on the job. In time he also hired three of his patrilineal cousins. Job skills and job recruitment occur through other kin networks as well, particularly among affines of "close family" members. Nevertheless, localized patrilineal descent groups seem to be particularly important among families who have skills, connections with whites, and other resources.

Although skilled construction work is the best employment available for black men, workers face many difficulties on their jobs. Construction work offers little job security. Workers are subject to layoffs when business is slack. In addition, there is a great likelihood of injury on the job. Under present laws, employers are required to carry workman's compensation and insurance to cover workers in case of injury. In several instances, however, injured workers and their families have had to take legal action before employers would pay these benefits. Yet, because of the high demand for skilled workers in construction, men can find new jobs fairly easily if they are mistreated by an employer. Occasionally they are in a position to start their own contracting businesses. Many men in the community have formed business partnerships with their brothers, sons, and cousins. Many others hope to establish business ventures. Sam Jackson, 38, a carpenter, is trying to build up a business. Currently he works a regular job and takes side jobs on the weekend. He has built up a good clientele and sometimes makes as much money from contracting as he does on his weekday job. He plans to work a few more years and then go into business with his son.

For the men of Sam's generation, the postwar growth in the construction industry enhanced job opportunities and introduced a degree of flexibility that did not earlier exist. When Ike Simmons, Sr., entered the job market in the 1930s, jobs were very scarce. Expansion in the area was just beginning as northern developers and speculators were buying failing plantations. Ike got a job on a nearby island resort where he and his father and brothers had supplied fish for years. Under new ownership the island's development expanded, and Ike was put in charge of installing and maintaining waterworks. Ike's job was demanding work for which he got little pay or recognition.

> I put in the water works on that island, know all about them things. Had a whole crew of men under me. I was the main person on that island. They depend on me for everything. Sometime I come to work on Monday and the weight of the water tank be way up to the top. Well that tank be nearly dry, and everybody complaining about they water running low. They didn't know how to back wash a well or nothing. They just look to me for everything. So I get a gang of men together and we go fixing. Foreman would come up to me and say, "Ike, I sho' glad you here. I hope you don't never leave this island." But when the big bossman come, he don't say nothing about me. And I ain't got paid nothing neither.

When Ike finally quit his job in 1969, because of deteriorating health, he was being paid $1.40 an hour. Wages for skilled construction work today range from $4.00 to $8.00 an hour.

While employment opportunities for black men have increased somewhat with industrial development, jobs for black women remain scarce. The most common sources of employment for women are domestic work, farm work, and maintenance work in resort motels and restaurants. These jobs are low-paying, menial, and hold no future beyond the scant daily wage. Women refer to these jobs as "hard work," "working out," and "working for nothing."

For these reasons, the women of Mt. Pleasant have created work alternatives for themselves outside of wage labor. Over 50 percent of the Mt. Pleasant women produce baskets that they sell to tourists from makeshift, wooden stands along the coastal highway that passes through the community.[5] These highway basket stands are operated by collectives of kinswomen: women and their daughters, two or more sisters and their daughters, and sometimes cousins and nonkin as well. The core of this cooperative unit, however, is usually made up of women who are "close family," women who cooperate in both domestic and work activities. Women organize their daily schedules by dividing up these tasks: who will go to the basket stand that day, who will keep the children, who will take a sick child to the clinic, who will collect baskets from other kinswomen, and so on.

The tradition of basket-making has been handed down from mother to daughter for generations. Originally baskets were made for agricultural use. When car travel and tourism began in the 1920s, women began making "show baskets" using different materials and emphasizing aesthetic designs. With the growth of tourism in the last twenty years, the basket-making business has expanded considerably.

For the older women of Mt. Pleasant, the basket-making trade is an extension of their tradition as independent producers and entrepreneurs. For example, Mrs. Edna Rouse, now in her seventies, produced and marketed vegetables and flowers for most of her life. As these productive activities were displaced, she turned her entrepreneurial and craft skills to basket-making. She conducts a thriving business with the help of her daughters and granddaughters. She has also participated in many craft shows, including exhibits at the Smithsonian Institution. She prides herself in these accomplishments and in her determination as an independent producer and businesswoman. "If I just got two baskets, I'll come down here and sell them myself, and that will be the money I have. I make what I have off my own thing. I work domestic for a while but mostly I been selling my vegetable and basket. Selling and buying, that's me. I can get my own money with my own two hand. Then I know they ain't no cheating going on."

For the younger women engaged in basket-making, the harsh reality, however, is having limited employment options. Many of the younger women turned to basket-making after searching in vain for jobs that "pay something." The work history of Edith, aged 35, is typical for women of her generation. Edith worked off and on as a domestic, a farm worker, and a maintenance worker in local motels while her children were young. Once they reached school age and her husband began to make more money on his job, Edith started looking for full-time work. She tried to get a job as a city bus driver, but was unsuccessful; she considered training as an auto mechanic, but could not afford to go to school; she applied for a job as a nurse's aide, but was told she could not get that position without previous experience. Disappointed and angry, Edith finally gave up, but rather than continue working at menial labor jobs, she set up a highway basket stand with her sister. "These job around here, you don't make nothing. Working these place around here I make $60 a week. Then they take out tax and social security. You bring home $50 for a whole week work. You look at that paycheck and you want to cry. So, I just decided to go with these same basket here, and I'll stick with that."

For the women of Mt. Pleasant, the best possibility for employment is the Medical University complex. There are five hospitals in Charleston, and they employ over 1,000 people. Of approximately 600 nonprofessional workers, two-thirds are black women (Hoffius, n.d.). Most employed women between the ages of 30 and 50 work at the Medical University. Without previous experience, however, these jobs are difficult to obtain. With two exceptions, the women who hold these jobs had previous hospital experience in New York.

Many women, unable to get job training and jobs, migrate to New York City in search of employment. In New York, the competition for unskilled jobs, particularly hospital work, is not as great, and the requirements are not as rigorous as they are in South Carolina. Women in New York who already have employment in hospitals recruit interested kin from South Carolina. When previous job experience is required, kinswomen sometimes provide this as well. In at least two cases, women's "previous job experience" consisted of crash courses on hospital procedures given them by kinswomen. Women who have received job experience in New York stand a far better chance of getting similar jobs in Charleston.

The other advantage of work in New York is the experience gained in large workplaces where unions and grievance procedures are a matter of course. Women return to Charleston with a keener awareness of how to handle difficulties on the job. Elsa, for example, worked in the dietary department of a large New York hospital. When she returned to Charleston, she got a comparable job in a local hospital. "When I came back South, I told myself two things—I ain't working for chicken feed and I ain't taking any shit on the job. I been around and I know how things are supposed to be."

Although women who have been to New York acquire experience and skills in negotiating employee-employer relations, the determination to demand respect and adequate wages is nothing new to the black women of Mt. Pleasant. They are attempting to bargain for a respected position in wage labor jobs that they once held as farmers and entrepreneurs. The productive roles of women are important to their social status as adults. An important dimension of social adulthood for both men and women in Mt. Pleasant is individual autonomy and self-sufficiency. Black women take offense at the suggestion, for example, that they are financially dependent on their husbands: "My husband don't support me! I support myself. I don't have to beg a man for money." Women expect to work and to help support the household and children.

Employment away from home, however, imposes an added burden on women with young children. This burden is considerably alleviated by cooperative arrangements between kinswomen. The first question women asked me (assuming that I had children) was, "Is your mother living? Girl, when my mother was living, I ain't had nothing to worry about." Many arrangements are made to accommodate the needs of children while women work, whether in Charleston or New York. Most changes in household residence involve child-care arrangements.

But children are not viewed as impediments to employment. As women see it, the obstacles are low wages, menial labor, and dead-end jobs. The women of Mt. Pleasant hope to better life's prospects for their sons and daughters. Their hopes rest on changing opportunities for blacks in employment and education. For the young men and women presently seeking employment, desegregation policies have made some differences in job possibilities. The better jobs, however, usually require some form of higher education, either vocational training or college. Local educational facilities are inadequate for present demands, and college is expensive. Few families can afford higher education for their children.

The families with children in college have accomplished this with the financial assistance of kin. Irene has three children attending the black state college at Orangeburg, South Carolina. She is divorced and works as a nurse's aide. Her eleven brothers and sisters have helped her to provide for her four children and send them to school. "All eleven head of us brothers and sisters are really tight. If I can't do something for my kids, my brothers and sisters will. If I can't go pick up one of the kids from school, Al just jumps in his car and goes to get them. My kids have gotten a little spoiled in that way. They know there will always be one of us—if not me, then one of my brothers and sisters—to help them out and do for them." Cooperative bonds in educating young adults also can be seen within the context of the natal family. Parents may educate one son or daughter with the expectation that he or she, in turn, will help finance the education of another sibling. This was the arrangement in Lea and Sam Johnson's household. Lea and Sam sent their son to law school while they both held full-time jobs in Florida. Their son now has a good job and is sending his younger sister to nursing school.

Reciprocity and mutual responsibility are cultural expectations in relations between kin and family members. These highly localized bonds of kinship based on patrimony in land and a shared community have allowed the black people of Mt. Pleasant to create alternative livelihoods to menial labor jobs and limited occupational mobility, and to acquire skills and education in the hope of obtaining better jobs. Lack of economic opportunity is the most apparent and immediate problem blacks face in their struggle for a place in the larger society. The greater obstacle is powerlessness in the political and economic structures that dominate their lives. Throughout their history, the blacks of Mt. Pleasant have utilized their resources and their kin and community networks to protect and defend themselves against the powerful elite. In their own communities they have maintained strong social boundaries and have effectively governed their own social relations through the complementary structures of religion and kinship—institutions referred to as "outside the law," that is, white law or "unjust law" (Guthrie 1977). The elders in kin groups and in the church not only governed internal community relations, but also mediated relations between the community and white-dominated institutions (Woofter 1930).

While the formal authority of community-based institutions has diminished in recent decades, the solidarity of kin and community is still the primary support for Mt. Pleasant blacks in their dealings with the law, medical and welfare institutions, and employers. When Anna had to appear in court concerning her daughter, for example, she recruited her mother, her two adult daughters, five brothers and sisters, two cousins, a community religious leader, and me. Appearing in the courtroom with all of her kin and friends was one way in which Anna influenced the court hearing. While awaiting the judge's decision, we all stood waiting in the hall outside the judge's chamber. Rosa Lee, the religious leader, held a prayer meeting. After she finished praying, everyone continued to stand in the hall. After an hour or so, I asked Anna why we did not find some place to sit down. "No, that wouldn't be smart. We'll stay right here so they won't forget us." The judge noticed this large gathering and became quite friendly and even accommodating. After four hours of patient waiting, Anna's daughter was ordered released from custody.

Since the enactment of civil rights legislation, the blacks of Mt. Pleasant have begun to seek legal and political remedies for the discrimination and exploitation that they face in relations with white-dominated institutions. Many families, for example, have brought legal action on behalf of kin members against employers and state institutions. In large industrial workplaces, the problems faced by individual employees have been taken up by co-workers as well as families and communities.

The most significant campaign of this kind was the Charleston Hospital Strike of 1969, during which 400 blacks—nearly all women—walked off their jobs. In the months of struggle and repressive military action that ensued, the hospital workers gained national recognition and received the support of labor, civil rights, and civil liberties groups. That summer, 12,000 people marched through the streets of Charleston in support of the strikers. The black community sustained and supported the workers during these months. The local Longshoreman's Union, one of the oldest black unions in the country, threatened to close down the Charleston port unless the strike was settled favorably. Hoffius (n.d.) writes: "The community stood by the workers. When the workers finally walked out, the Medical University was unable to find many scab replacements."

The blacks of Mt. Pleasant share a heritage of resistance as slaves (Wood 1974), as freedmen (Dubois 1935; Williamson 1965), as peasant farmers (Mintz 1974), and as workers in an industrial economy. They have used whatever means available to create and maintain a material base for a social and religious community (Mintz and Price 1976). Throughout their history, the supportive networks of kin and community have been an important dimension in blacks' strategies of survival and resistance (Stack 1974; Gutman 1976). For the blacks of Mt. Pleasant, kinship is the idiom of solidarity and support: "My family is me. Anything you do to them, you do to me."

The importance of kin networks in the industrial context has been recognized by many scholars. What I see in Mt. Pleasant corroborates Stack's research (1974) among urban blacks in the United States and Bott's findings (1957) on the English working class; both demonstrate the significant role played by kin in providing care, support, and mutual aid among poor and working-class families. Scott and Tilly (1978) and other social historians (notably Anderson 1972 and Hareven 1978) have documented the active role of kin in helping individuals adjust to industrial conditions. This work also adds to the growing awareness among anthropologists and historians studying the southern working class—black and white—that kin and community also play central roles in active resistance movements (Friedman 1978; Hall 1980; Karen Sacks, personal communication). Women have figured significantly in these strategies of resistance, since it is they who have been relegated to secondary status and who have been displaced in the transition to wage labor (Boserup 1970; Caulfield 1974). The participation of men, women, and their kin in these larger struggles for reform at least suggests the process through which kin-based social relations become political means for coping with the exigencies of being black, working class, and, for half of the population, female.

NOTES

All of the personal names used in this paper are fictitious. This work has benefited from the comments and support of many friends and colleagues. Extensive dialogues with Jacquelyn Hall and Karen Sacks on their research with working-class blacks and whites were invaluable in developing the framework presented herein. Carol Stack's abiding interest, guidance, and careful prodding provided the impetus for reformulating my approach to this research. Leon Fink and Sue Levine have helped illuminate this subject in the context of labor history and southern labor movements. Sydney Nathan's extensive comments and criticisms were instrumental in preparing this paper for publication. The Rockefeller Foundation provided financial support for both my research and writing.

1. This figure is based on a sample survey of 92 households.
2. *Family* in this context is a general term used by Mt. Pleasant people to refer to all recognized kin.
3. Heavy pressures are now being exerted by the local county planning board to subdivide family land into individual house plots. This new policy is causing considerable concern because it further erodes the authority of old people, and is in direct opposition to Mt. Pleasant blacks' concepts of property as a right, not a possession or commodity.
4. This figure is based on a survey of 35 men.
5. This figure is based on a survey of 57 women.

REFERENCES

Anderson, Michael, 1972. *Family Structure in Nineteenth-Century Lancashire* (Cambridge: Cambridge University Press).
Bethel, Elizabeth Rauh, 1981. *Promiseland: A Century of Life in a Negro Community* (Philadelphia: Temple University Press), in press.
Boserup, Ester, 1970. *Women's Role in Economic Development* (New York: St. Martin's Press).

Bott, Elizabeth, 1957. *Family and Social Network* (New York: The Free Press).

Caulfield, Mina Davis, 1974. Imperialism, the Family, and Cultures of Resistance. *Socialist Revolution* 20:67–86.

DuBois, W. E. B., 1935. *Black Reconstruction in America* (New York: Russell-Russell).

Friedman, Elizabeth, 1978. Working paper on file, Center for the Study of the Family and the State, Duke University.

Guthrie, Patricia, 1977. Rights of Plantation Members: An Analysis of Praise House Worship and Litigation among "Gullah" Blacks of St. Helena, South Carolina. Paper presented at the 77th Annual Meeting of the American Anthropological Association, San Francisco.

Gutman, Herbert G., 1976. *The Black Family in Slavery and Freedom, 1750–1925* (New York: Pantheon).

Hall, Jacquelyn Dowd, 1980. The Elizabethton, Tennessee, Strike of 1929: Anatomy of a Research Project. Paper presented as part of Women's Week, University of South Florida, Tampa.

Hareven, Tamara K., 1978. Dynamics of Kin in an Industrial Community. *American Journal of Sociology*, special supplement, 4:180–92.

Hoffius, Steve, n.d. 1969 Charleston Hospital Worker's Strike. In *Working Lives*, Mark Miller, ed. (New York: Pantheon), in press.

Kiser, Clyde Vernon, 1969. *Sea Island to City* (New York: Atheneum).

Mintz, Sidney M., 1974. *Caribbean Transformations* (Chicago: Aldine).

Mintz, Sidney M., and Richard Price, 1976. An Anthropological Approach to the Afro-American Past: A Caribbean Perspective. 2 *ISHI* Occasional Papers in Social Change (Philadelphia: Institute for the Study of Human Issues).

Murray, Chalmers S., 1949. *This Our Land* (Columbia, S.C.: R. L. Bryan).

Rose, Willie Lee, 1964. *Rehearsal for Reconstruction* (New York: Vintage Books).

Scott, Joan, and Louise Tilly, 1978. *Women, Work, and Family* (New York: Holt, Rinehart, and Winston).

Stack, Carol B., 1974. *All Our Kin: Strategies for Survival in a Black Community* (New York: Harper and Row).

Tindall, George Brown, 1952. *South Carolina Negroes: 1877–1900* (Columbia: University of South Carolina Press).

Williamson, Joel, 1965. *After Slavery* (Chapel Hill: University of North Carolina Press).

Wood, Peter H., 1974. *Black Majority* (New York: W. W. Norton).

Woofter, Thomas J., 1930. *Black Yeomanry: Life of St. Helena Island* (New York: Henry Holt).

The Contradictions of a Kinship Community

ALLEN BATTEAU

Our image of the peripheral sectors of the American world system is at times inappropriately cast in terms of premodern communities under the domination of the metropolitan center. The forces of colonial domination, in such a view, are seen to be appropriating the economic resources and destroying the cultural integrity of the traditional community. The great validity that this model has had in examining the confrontation of American and non-Western societies does not consistently obtain on the internal periphery. Here, the dependent system may itself contain contradictions and conflicts which determine and are determined by the historical transformations in its relationship to the metropolis. Such is the case, I would like to suggest, for certain communities in eastern Kentucky. (Cf. Wallerstein 1974 on the concept of a world system; and Walls 1978 for its application to Appalachia.)

To examine the various parts of local groupings in terms of their dynamic relationship to each other and to their political environment is hardly a novel enterprise for anthropologists. Leach (1954) has demonstrated for the Burmese Kachin that kinship groups were not isolated from surrounding ethnic groups, and that the articulation of subordinate and dominant groups through intermarriage and assimilation decisively affected the control of one by the other. Studies of interchanges across local and ethnic boundaries are well known, and the maintenance of ethnic identities in the face of intermarriage and other pressures toward assimilation is a frequently observed process (cf. Dominguez 1977, for instance). In modern societies, however, there is a new set of problems relating to local kinship and kinlike structures, and their external political relationships. The normative separation of civil society from domestic relationships precludes the use of kinship structures as instruments of policy (as was the case for the Kachin); corresponding to this, ethnic groups are not politically articulated, and clear ethnic boundaries are enforced only through discrimination or through a self-conscious process of enclave formation. Where such clear boundaries between local groupings and the larger society do not exist, the observable interpenetration of civil and domestic relationships, in the face of their normative separation, becomes a major issue for research. This issue has been evaded in American and Appalachian studies by examining localities in isolation—"community studies"—or by inflating the symbols of local identity into markers of ethnic boundaries.

This discussion will suggest an alternative approach by examining a kinship community in the mountains of eastern Kentucky. This community is a political unit in which the predominant forms of solidarity are either contained within or patterned after kinship relationships. This state of affairs is idealized by local statements such as, "We're all kin around here." It is similarly idealized by regional advocates who state that, in the face of "outside" influences, "the family and family groups in neighborhoods become the center for 'underground' mountain culture" (Lewis et al. 1978:131). Yet because of its overt political content and context, the kinship system so idealized contains numerous contradictions and conflicts, which I would summarize as a pattern of imbalanced factionalism. These contradictions are related to some of the unexpected results of the development of the region: the increasing wealth of the Appalachian gentry, the rise of new political machines, and the emergence of a new underclass as intractably poor as that which existed a hundred years ago. By examining social relationships within the community in terms of their distinctive pattern and contents, and the contradictions within and between these, we can correct for two perspectives that hitherto have dominated much of the literature of Appalachia: that of the particularists who see "Appalachia" as an ethnic entity with a unique culture (Jones 1975), and that of the developers who project a suburban future as a desirable goal for the mountain people of the South.

The initial formation of the southern mountain community was a product of the status that the migrant settlers had occupied on the eastern seaboard. Landless laborers and renters in a polity where land was the *sine qua non* of social standing seized the opportunity to own land, even if it meant a journey far from the existing centers of "civilization." Some well-connected settlers engrossed large tracts of tens of thousands of acres for speculative purposes; their successors, occupying the broad river bottoms and attempting plantation agriculture or mercantile enterprise, became the Appalachian gentry. For the most part, though, the settlers were small farmers, would-be yeomen, for whom acquiring land, however marginal, was a form of upward mobility. This mixed pattern in the initial acquisition of land, combining speculative engrossment of large tracts with the settlement of small holdings by the farmers, created a highly dispersed pattern of settlement with almost no nucleated villages. This settlement pattern has played a fateful role in Appalachian development ever since.

The historical data on the mountain community are, at best, contradictory. Some scholars, such as Emma B. Miles, noted the absence of community: "There is no such thing as a community of mountaineers. They are knit together, man to man, as friends, but not as a body of men" (quoted in Kephart 1922:384). Others take note of certain forms of community, such as religious meetings: "In no part of our country will one find a more deep and sincere interest in matters of religion than in the southern highlands. . . . [The mountaineer] is well disposed toward church, which he attends regularly or as regularly as is possible" (Campbell 1921:176 f.). One can only conclude that even in terms of *rural* social forms, "Appalachia" is a most diverse region: in various localities one can collect reports of what resemble endogamous demes and exogamous moieties (Matthews 1965; Karen Li Simpkins, personal communication), preferences for and proscriptions on cousin marriage (Brown 1952; Heller and Quesada 1977), as well as patrilineages and ambilineal ramages. My remarks, hence, will be understood to pertain, not to the region as a whole, but only to the farming districts adjacent to the coal fields of eastern Kentucky.

Within the area described here, localities can be characterized as kinship communities. It is not that every member is related to every other, but rather that in this local grouping most important activities either take place within kinship relationships, or else are patterned by the structure of kinship. The significant features of this structure, for present purposes, are a network of kinship relationships encompassing the entire community, and a conceptual map of named kinship segments, or *sets*. Identification with one kinship grouping or another forms a major part of an individual's reputation in the community. Other groupings and other forms of solidarity, such as labor unions and sectarian congregations, take their form from the pervasive idiom of kinship. The growth of industrial, commercial, and administrative activities has, to be sure, altered this, particularly along the main roads. Out in the "hollers," the cul-de-sacs branching off of the main roads, where formerly most of the population lived, one still finds this pattern in but slightly diluted form.

Activities that are exclusively contained within kinship groups include, of course, householding and the early years of child-raising; before the consolidation of schools, the later years of socialization were also subordinated to kinship groups, in that local groups exerted dominant influence over neighborhood one-room schools. Politics is predominately, although not exclusively, structured by kinship, with voting frequently based on kindred loyalty and family name. In political advertisements, the candidates stress not only their names, but the names of their parents, their spouse's parents, their grandparents' names, and their spouse's grandparents' names; if the candidate's wife has better local credentials, more mention will be made of *her* family and *her* people than of the candidate's own. To a variable extent, such matters as law enforcement, employment, and informal social participation are substantially affected by kinship. In some districts, church membership is recruited along kinship lines (Stephen Kane, personal communication); even where it is not, one can observe that the symbols of kinship and the symbols of church membership are in many ways isomorphic. Churches function as extended kinship groups, providing support in crises, emotional closeness, supervision of behavior, and one of the few places for self-expression in the community. This embeddedness and patterning justifies the term "kinship community."

In such a community, the most important dimensions of personal identity derive from kinship referents. After age and sex, family name is paramount: one of the first questions asked of a male stranger, even one well into adulthood, is, "Whose boy are you?" Having the right family name is more important than having a good credit rating at the bank—or more accurately, family name *is* one's credit rating at the bank.

To be sure, kinship is not the only form of social organization. People do have jobs in organizations that are nominally bureaucratic. Though the county sheriffs have traditionally owed their position to being part of one family or another, the state police are usually independent of such parochial ties. One should note, however, that parts of this region are legendary for the ineffectiveness or corruption of such organizations; this ineffectiveness—reflected in such matters as protection given to bootleggers, favoritism shown by courts, or nepotism in hiring—is in large part due to the strength of kinship loyalties.

In order to see how this system orders the lives of its members, we can look at its ideology, and the pattern of relationships and activities associated with it. The ideology of the kinship community is best expressed by the local statement, "We're all kin around here." The implications of this are not that there is a consanguineal or affinal link between everyone in the locality—although it requires only a few of these to unite all but a few visiting professionals. Rather, its meaning is that "we're all alike," as indicated by common participation in certain rituals and symbols that define local identity. Most of these are symbols of the hardships associated with "country" living: to say that "I was raised on soup beans and cornbread," like the expression "I've walked out of the holler many a morning," is to say, "I've had it rough; I'm an authentic mountain person." That many persons invoke these symbols only as a matter of ritual, while others use them as a matter of practical necessity, does not prevent the definition of a common identity on the basis of them. By transforming local relationships (people "around here") into kinship relationships ("We're all kin . . ."), this ideology supports the position of local elites as knowing "what's best for our people."

However, a careful examination of any locality reveals some definite fissures among the people who are "all kin around here." This is most noticeable in the identification of individuals with their parents and more distant ancestors: personalities, moral traits, and reputations, like names, are passed down from parents to children. This establishes a category of individuals that the mountain people call the "generation"—the descendants of a given ancestor, whether through males, females, or both. The local segment of a generation, particularly that of some ancestor who is well known, is called the "set." The set consists of those descendants of some original settler who live at or near the original homeplace. These are named collectivities, identified with particular places and particular ancestors: thus the Ball Creek Crocketts are distinguished from the Clear Creek Crocketts, and the Fiddler Shade *set* of Mosbys is distinguished from the Summer Jim *set* of Mosbys. Further, different sets have different reputations: on Ball Creek, I was told, there were two sets of Browns, one that was very tight and stingy, and one that was quite generous and accommodating. In rural localities where industrial and commercial development have made little headway, most people are identified with one set or another; along a main-road area of 419 households, I found through a comprehensive survey that better than 75 percent of the households were closely connected to one or another of 45 sets.[1]

This system is ordered by parentage, locality, and the corporate possession of a name. Other principles of organization, such as affinal and collateral relationships, are subsumed under these. Affines, "after they've lived with [i.e., near] you for a while," come to "seem like your own people." A married woman, having the maiden name of, say, Jones, will explain that she "really" is a Jones, even though her surname is currently Smith. Often lost sight of are collaterals, especially those more distant than second cousin or those living far away.

Conceptually, this system is segmentary, and the whole idea of segmentation provides some important insights into behavior within the system: the diffuse forms of social control, and the reputational competition, to be noted below, are typical of segmentary systems. Further, the residential pattern back in the hollows does closely fit the segmentary map. However, there are other areas of behavior that are little constrained by such segmental boundaries: cooperation in securing jobs, help with farming tasks, aid in crises, help in building a house, sales of land, political manipulation—all are influenced by far more considerations than simply identification with one set or another. When I conducted a close and comprehensive examination of three sets, I found very little interaction between most persons belonging to the same set unless they were siblings, siblings-in-law, or brothers and sisters in the church. Further, I found close friendships between nonrelatives, friendships involving cooperation in business dealings and politics; yet further, I found cases where members of the same set were not on speaking terms with each other. In other words, considered in terms of actual behavior beyond the establishment of residence, this system more resembles a network of relationships, many of them elective, than an array of segments. Connections in this network having instrumental content are as much a matter of friendship and personal preference as they are of name and parentage.

It is in conflict situations that the system begins to crystallize, particularly in the quadrennial primary elections. If a family gets "interested" in a particular race, it will first call on the support of all of its people living in the district—that is, all members of its set. The goal of such races, particularly those at the most local levels, is not so much the powers and perquisites of elected office; for magistrates and constables, these are minimal. Many seek election simply for the purpose of "making a name" for themselves. Efforts at "making a name," being a zero-sum game, immediately call into being opposition efforts, so that local politics takes on a decidedly factional quality. While some families and sets never get involved in this factional competition, others can be counted on, every four years, to jump into some local or county race.

These findings may be an artifact of the area I studied, and have little validity outside of eastern Kentucky. My general findings are of a conceptual map of named kinship segments, which function as resources for the formation of networks of reciprocity and friendship. These findings seem to be supported by the work of other scholars: examining a mountain farming community in the 1940s, James Brown found sets similar to those I found thirty years later. These sets ranged in size up to fifteen households; they contained "family groups" of two to four households, within which cooperation was quite intense (Brown 1952). In the 1970s in western North Carolina, Pat Beaver found the contrast between conceptual segmentation and an actual pattern of complex networks of cooperation (Beaver 1976). In the same period in eastern Tennessee, Carlene Bryant found a hilltop community made up of four family groups, ranging in size from five to twenty-two households; the boundaries and genealogies of these groups, she found, were adjusted to explain the realities of contemporary opposition and cooperation (Bryant 1979). All of this suggests that while local details may vary, there is some correspondence in the form of kinship in different parts of the southern Appalachian region.

Finally, one might consider the developmental history of families within these groupings. A clear majority of adults live outside of the neighborhood in which they were raised, although most households are located in the home neighborhood of one of their adult members. From a cross-sectional examination of the residential history of the families in my survey, it appeared that the typical mobility history was *not* to move out of a home neighborhood before marriage, and then return after marriage; rather, migration and return migration for those families that do return to the community occurred between marriage and the birth of the first child. For older families, there was no migration; the youngest families, the newly marrieds, were quite likely to be living near the husband's parents. After some moving about, they tended to divide evenly between husband's and wife's homeplace. Recognizing the hazards of drawing developmental conclusions from cross-sectional data, one can surmise that these sets are not fixed groups, but rather, represent a framework of relationships within which there are several choices to be exercised, at different points in the life cycle. The ends to be realized by these choices are culturally specified, and the structure of the community creates certain opportunities; the manner in which any given household adapts to and manipulates these over the course of its existence is determined by more contingent factors such as employment possibilities.

Descriptively, there are two aspects of this system emphasized here: one is its formal plan, its blueprint, which entails a strong identification with family and homeplace and strong obligations of solidarity toward kin. The other aspect is the actual fluidity and flexibility of the pattern of social relationships. The net result of this is a system that is fairly successful at distributing scarcity among its members: hardships are shared, and nobody goes hungry on account of misfortune. The incidence of poverty, however, is directly related to this feature: for it is families who are cut off from these networks, from this sharing, that experience chronic poverty, meaning both economic scarcity and personal demoralization. A son who is estranged from his parents and siblings, a daughter who was abandoned by her widowed father when he remarried, are the sorts of persons who are permanently poor.

Conversely, the reciprocity expected in kinship relationships does not observably hinder the economic advancement of families, as has been reported in other localities marked by intensive poverty. In contrast to groups whose position as minority enclaves is pronounced, these families are expected to share only the barest requirements of subsistence. In a midwestern black community, Stack (1974) found that claims for money were made on anyone with sudden good fortune; I found none of this in eastern Kentucky. One was expected to share food, clothing, tools perhaps, with those who needed them to survive; access to a job was also frequently sought from kinsmen. But cash for leisure or funds for capital investment were neither sought nor offered. Families whose economic success is particularly outstanding are targets of envy, gossip, political intrigue, and occasional requests for assistance, but such efforts do not threaten these families' economic position. The immobilization of the poor in Appalachia, instead, derives from a different state of affairs: in addition to the double binds and demoralization of the welfare system, there is a public stigma attached to receiving welfare, thus permanently marking one as "lazy, no-count," and closing off access to many possible jobs. That such stigmatized identities are internalized, and the demoralization accepted, is testimony to the effectiveness of the system.

There are some troubling data that seem to contradict the ideology of "We're all kin" and the norms of neighborly solidarity. We might note, for example, the great inequalities of wealth in this area: in the district in which I conducted a survey, the top quintile, or one-fifth, of households held 45 percent of the district's taxable wealth, while the bottom quintile controlled only 4.5 percent. The wealthiest set had an average wealth per household of $25,000, while the poorest had only $500 per household. One need only note the contrast between Pond Branch, with its row of brick homes with Cadillacs in front and swimming pools in back, and Mosby Fork, where dilapidated wood houses are crowded closely together, with dirt-bare front yards and propped-up pickup trucks, to appreciate the degree of inequality within this area; further east, in the heart of the coal-mining districts, it is even greater.

A second sort of datum that seems at odds with the notion of "We're all kin" is the disavowal of kinship occasionally found. For instance, there are two sets of Shifletts in the county that I studied. Although they are descended from a common ancestor, Bill Shiflett, and are named after two of his sons, they do not claim any kinship to each other. One of these sets is often stigmatized as having a disreputable life style, while the other includes some of the leading citizens of the county. Methods for breaking kinship relationships include moving away from a district, simply not claiming someone as kin, or the extreme of an alteration in the spelling of one's surname—from *Owsley* to *Ousley*, or *Shiflett* to *Schifflette*—to signify the change in status.

Finally, one might note the factional tendencies in local politics. Factionalism is nothing new in kin-based societies, although within segmentary systems, properly speaking, there is the expectation that local factions will merge in the face of outside threats and split only for internal quarrels. But in eastern Kentucky local factions will often form alliances with outside groups, whether strip miners, land speculators, or church missionaries. The dominant families in the county polity are well known for which of the various factions in the state Democratic Party they are allied and identified with. Less powerful families at times throw in with strip mine operators or university-educated community organizers. Whether all of this is "selling out" or "forming a strategic alliance" seems to depend on where one stands.

This cooperation between local groups and "outside" developers has deep historical roots in eastern Kentucky. In every form of major development—whether the introduction of a cash economy with the development of logging, the creation of an industrial regime in the mining camps, the improvement of education, or the new forms of dependency brought by the welfare state—the pioneering entrepreneurs were not outsiders, but locally born and raised mountaineers from such towns as Hazard and Paintsville. The outside predation and expropriation of Appalachia is an uncontrovertible fact; but in every case, the ground was broken for it by local persons such as John C.C. Mayo and Bascom Slemp. Similarly today, the Appalachian Regional Commission, whose efforts are viewed ambivalently by many in the region, was initiated by a group of businessmen from the towns of eastern Kentucky.

All of these observations suggest something other than a bounded system in functional equilibrium. To reconcile these with the ideology and demonstrable intensity of kinship in the community, we must refract the local system into its constituent domains of pure kinship, personal identity, householding, and child-raising. Each of these has its own set of symbols, values, and norms which most of the people in the region clearly understand. It is not my analytic device to separate these so much as it is our professional rhetoric to call their aggregation a "kinship system."

If we stop thinking in terms of systems and institutions, and instead focus on what our informants are thinking about, we find that they use certain objects, ideas, and symbols to order their lives. A mundane object such as a house, in addition to its practical functions of keeping the weather out and providing a place to sleep, has a host of symbolic messages which, when understood, tell us much about why mountain people order their domestic lives as they do. A nuclear family occupies the house, and it is thought improper for more than one family to live under one roof. The household is very tightly bounded: strangers, including fieldworkers, have to be very careful about how they approach the house, go through the front gate, step on the porch, or cross the threshold. The house is the normal place for eating meals, and very rarely will unrelated families sit down together at the same table to eat. It is a symbol of status and prestige: owning a home is preferable to being "just a renter," for the homeowner and landowner is therefore independent; as one fellow put it to me, "He has land that he can be independent on." As a symbol of status, one's house should not be too close to another's; it is a symbol of dependency to live in a house out behind someone else's and a symbol of low prestige to live in a tight cluster of country houses. The condition and construction materials of the house also say much about one's prestige in the community. Having said all of this, I should repeat my earlier observation, that in the early years of marriage, children often live close to the husband's parents, and that the typical living arrangement is for parents to have some of their children living in houses clustered around their own, in a small hamlet. In such hamlets, as one patriarch put it, "Me and the old woman and the girls, we kindly live through and through one another. What one's got, the other's got."

This is the domain of householding—a set of relationships based on co-residence, commensality, and fixity of place. Its emphasis is on independence, sharing within an independent unit; yet the continued dependence within a family, carrying through even to the establishment of new domestic units, is also clear. Also clear is the manner in which this domain interpenetrates with the economic position of the family, in terms of the manner in which house and land are obtained.

We can see how this domain of householding contrasts with the domain of "pure" kinship. "Pure" kinship emphasizes solidarity between all persons related by blood and marriage and a certain identification with them; householding emphasizes independence. The conjunction of the two is in the structure of the hamlet, in which the children's homes may be as little as ten yards away from the parents' yet still be structurally separate. The disjunction between the two can be seen in the manner in which relationships even between parents and children are attenuated, sometimes seemingly forgotten, when children move away from their parents and make no effort to see them.

A related domain is that of filiation. This is the relationship that is established by being "raised up" by another person. Here the emphasis is not on sharing but on giving, creating an obligation that can never be fully repaid. "Raising up" is done by taking care of the child and teaching it the proper way to live. The preferred context for this is within the nuclear family, because it is felt that a child needs both a mother and a father who can be counted on to have a "natural" affection for it. The great valuation of kin relationships within this community has, in the past, led to rather sizeable families—families with as many as ten children were not uncommon fifty years ago. These characteristics of the Appalachian family tend to elicit personality traits that are, at times, at odds with some of the normative emphases of other domains. For instance, the typical household consisting of a large number of children living in close quarters is perforce emotionally intense: children growing up in such an environment learn to be very sensitive to the feelings, wishes, and opinions of others. This is reflected later in life in the elaborate gestures of courtesy by which disagreements between friends or kin are handled: "Now, this is just the way I feel," as I heard one fellow say in a small group; "You can do with it what you like. I don't mean nothing against nobody by it. I've just been studying on the matter, and this is how I feel." It is consistent with the extreme measures taken to avoid open conflicts within groups, which Hicks (1976:88 ff.) terms the "ethic of neutrality." Such traits should suggest a more complex portrait of personality traits within the region than the simple characterizations of "independence" and "individualism" that have dominated the literature (see Erikson 1976:77 f. for an elaboration on this). Yet further, a typical development history is of extreme indulgence for the baby of the family (that is, the youngest member), followed by the abrupt termination of attention and nurturance when the next child comes along. This pattern of socialization, which is part of what Eric Wolf characterizes as "dependency training" (Wolf 1966), is adapted to a setting where adults are expected to become parts of groups already in existence rather than striking out on their own.

From such "raising up" is created a lifelong obligation towards, and an emotional dependence on, whoever raised the child. Further, the child learns that he should not "get above his raisings," that is, exhibit a style of life markedly more affluent than the one with whom he was raised. Economic advancement is acceptable so long as one does not flaunt it when coming back home, either in dress or speech or the way one sits in a chair, or even in the food one eats. "Getting above your raisings" is in the end a denial of kinship, by asserting a status claim within the family: either the family will attempt to gainsay the status claim through ridicule or gossip, or kinship will be denied. (This subordination of kinship to status identities is further evident in the endogamy of status categories, and in the political manipulation of status identities in order to create an illusion of kinship with constituents; cf. Batteau 1978, pt. 4.) One might further note in passing that several moral and personal attributes are associated with "raising up": "I was raised a Democrat," "I wasn't raised to drink no whiskey," or "I was raised on soup beans and cornbread" are not so much statements of one's biography as they are statements of one's values.

A central domain is that of personal identity, symbolized by the distinct name that one has. A name is both a label and a reputation. As a reputation, a name emphasizes two matters. First, it stresses the moral qualities that one *shares* with neighbors, kinsmen, and family. One person's misdemeanor can give his entire family a bad name. As noted previously, different kinship groups are said to have different moral traits—the Ryans are tight, the Slones are good livers, the Adamsons are industrious, the Pratts are solid citizens, the Elkins are ruthless, and the Houghs are good-natured. I noted previously that two sets of Browns were said by some not to be kin, and that they had different moral traits attributed to them; this difference in the moral heritage of the two sets was explained to me as being due to the fact that one of the eponymous Browns had married a Ryan, while the other had married a Hough. In fact, categories of kinship at times become categories of morals, as when Faulkner says that Eck Snopes was "never in this world a Snopes."

Further, qua reputation, a name emphasizes one's own personal achievements—having a "big name"—achievements that set one *apart* from neighbors and distant kin. In the opportunities for making a big name, there is an important intersection with politics: one of the major opportunities for a person to make a name for himself and his people is by beating opponents in local politics.

This dual interchangeability of moral and political identities on the one hand, and kinship identities on the other, is one of the most important aspects of this system. It creates a set of motivations in which family obligations and relationships are orchestrated to reinforce social order through pressures to maintain a good name, through the breaking of family and local ties and the creation and reinforcement of social boundaries when these pressures fail, and through the channeling of ambition and ego-enhancement into the socially acceptable direction of building up a kinship group.

From the exposition thus far, one can sense certain conflicting norms and contradictory definitions—between the independence emphasized in house-holding and the dependence emphasized in filiation; between the solidarity emphasized through the norms of kinship, the shared quality of relationships, and the personal advancement implicit in making a name; between the forms of kinship solidarity and the means available for breaking kinship; and be-tween the stratification of the community and the notion that "we're all kin."

The basic datum for understanding these contradictions is the stratification of the community. Externally, this stratification is based on the fact that the community participates in a competitive economy, which by its very nature distributes rewards unequally. However, the dynamic of the settlement pattern supports this stratification as well. As I previously stated, children tend to settle at or near the homeplace of their parents or in-laws, if they settle in the community at all. A frequently stated ideal is for the parents' home to be sur-rounded by the homes of their offspring. Many parents build such houses around their own, while others deed their children homesites, perhaps holding out the valued prospect of inheriting the old homeplace, in order to persuade the children to remain close to home. Given the fact that children do marry, however, no more than half can settle at the old homeplace; some must move off to the spouse's homeplace, if not out of the community altogether. As it turns out, some families are more successful than others in keeping their chil-dren close to home. These turn out to be the families with more advantages— the better-reputed, the wealthier, and the better-connected. If one takes all of the sets in the district surveyed and arranges them by who gives spouses to whom, one finds a fairly univalent rank ordering of the sets that has a strong positive correlation with family wealth ($r = +0.64$), officeholding, and land-ownership. This ability to attract in-marrying spouses, in turn, reinforces the position of the higher set, since the more kin a person has close at hand, the greater his prestige, his social resources, and hence his political power. The kinship system provides an important reinforcement for the system of economic and political stratification; this is consistent with Marshall Sahlins' observation (1961) that while segmentary lineage systems tend to be egalitar-ian, systems of non-unilineal groupings support the emergence of an elite.

Juxtaposed to this stratification is the previously noted factionalism of the community, based on intense family loyalties and the emphasis on having a big name through political success. Since having a big name is a zero-sum game, efforts at making a name through politics call into being opposition efforts. Focused on differentially ranked sets, the factions do not cut across the pattern of stratification within the community in any permanent fashion. There do exist alliances of political loyalty and expediency between the less and the more powerful families, ties which span the entire range of the community, so that one can find no clear dividing line between the "grass roots" and the "power structure." These alliances, however, are continually shifting, a fact that gives politics a bad name. The peripheral membership of any given faction is always quite fluid; the core is a family group in this system of stratified family groups.

The result is a local system of *imbalanced factionalism*. Certain dominant families, with kinship connections ramifying throughout the county, have maintained control over most important positions in the elections of this century. Through a latticework of neighborhood and kinship connections, forming alliances with other families, this control is articulated: when a town politician seeks votes, he calls on his friends out in the countryside; when a school superintendent pursues a program of school consolidation, a fundamental consideration is the use of his connections to create and maintain support for consolidation in the neighborhoods that will be losing schools. Within the county, such families control not only the political positions but many of the administrative ones as well: school officials, welfare officials, and (to a lesser extent) public safety officials are drawn from the leading families of the county. It would be misleading, however, to characterize these families as "brokers" or "gatekeepers" in their role of introducing outside resources, authority, and information into the local system. There is sufficient continuity and articulation between the lowland and the highland gentry to make the boundedness of the local system questionable: these two attend the same universities, they marry amongst each other, they are partners in the industrial development of the region, and there is sufficient mobility among this stratum from the highlands to the lowlands, and vice versa, to make it difficult to say where the "local system" ends and the "outside system" begins.[2] If one examines the history of eastern Kentucky counties, one finds, even in the years of most isolation, from 1870 to 1890, a constant ebb and flow of the rural gentry to the lowland centers, and vice versa.

At the other extreme of the rural social scale are the most desperately poor families of eastern Kentucky. These contain the parents who are fated to see their children move off after marriage, either for the city or for the homeplace of more affluent in-laws. Genealogically, these families have more kin in the community than others (because of their higher birth rate); socially, they have fewer resources because so many of their kin move off, avoid them, or perhaps even disclaim them. They are avoided and disclaimed because of the moral stigma attached to their poverty; the contagion of moral reputations, noted previously, means that one must avoid persons who, if the relationship were too actively maintained, might give one a bad name. Future research might question whether the newer forms of discrimination visited upon these families through the welfare system are more demoralizing or less than the collective hardships of earlier times: when the community was less stratified, kin ties provided a means of sharing hardships; today, similar ties are broken to form boundaries in the stratification system, when a moral distinction is added to an economic difference.

This is the final contradiction that I seek to emphasize: that despite the great valuation given to kinship and attachment to place, and despite the tangled web of kinship connections encompassing the entire community, this rural grouping is as differentiated as any other rural community; and further, the rhetoric of kinship supports the system of stratification, both through its dynamics of household formation and location, and through an ideology which legitimates the monopolies of the local gentry and stigmatizes the position of the poor. Within the system of stratification, the styles and rhetoric of kinship color relationships—supporting paternalism from above, and dependence and approval-seeking from below. Yet this Appalachian gentry, for all the rhetoric of "we're all kin," merges imperceptibly into the lowland gentry of the state. Either in terms of relationships or ideology, there is no singular boundary between the kinship system of this eastern Kentucky community and that of the rural South generally; this is not the kinship system of a bounded social entity, whether regional or ethnic, but simply the kinship system of our country cousins.

It is an abiding vice of anthropological research, with its reliance on ethnographic methods, to attempt to reproduce the tribe (or its epistemological equivalent) in every field situation. In modern societies, where local boundaries are increasingly effaced and the different contents of ethnic boundaries become progressively dubious, distinctions between internal and external relationships, like distinctions between domestic and civil spheres, frequently have but ideological validity. Only by examining such local and ethnic entities in their larger social and political context, and by focusing on the historical processes related to that context, can the ethnography of modern communities contribute to an ethnology of modern societies.

NOTES

Research for this paper was supported by a grant from the National Institute of Mental Health, #RO3-MH-31948, which is gratefully acknowledged. Support for the writing of this paper from a fellowship from the National Endowment for the Humanities is also gratefully acknowledged. I would like to express my appreciation to Susan Rodgers, Dennis Shepherd, Carol Stack, and Melinda Wagner for their perceptive comments and criticisms of an earlier draft of the paper; and to the Department of Anthropology of the University of Virginia for providing a most agreeable environment for its preparation. My observations are similar to those of James Brown, whose interest in Appalachian kinship has provided a guide and a stimulus for the research here presented.

1. This survey was conducted over a period of four weeks in January 1975. The neighborhood chosen was selected for containing the entire range of differentiation found within the county under study, and for being centered on a main road. Questions asked included household composition, occupation, educational levels, ancestry, residential history, and church membership; other data gathered included the type of house a family lived in, and their assessed taxable wealth. Additional details of this survey can be found in Batteau 1978.

2. To make the point schematically, one could distinguish between different groups such as the Appalachian yeomanry, the Appalachian proletariat, the Appalachian gentry, the Bluegrass gentry, and the Bluegrass aristocracy. Yet in terms of any *objective* measure of social boundaries, these groups merge imperceptibly into each other, forming a continuum whose topography is determined by subjective identification and stereotyping. The clearest boundaries within this continuum are not between these subjective status groupings, but within the yeomanry, who form local groups on the basis of place of origin and settlement. For a partial demonstration of this, see Batteau 1978:133. There is some evidence that this pattern is more common in Kentucky, where counties are smaller and big business interests less well entrenched, than it is in other Appalachian states.

REFERENCES

Batteau, Allen, 1978. *Class and Status in an Egalitarian Community* (Ph.D. diss., University of Chicago).

Beaver, Patricia D., 1976. *Symbols and Social Organization in an Appalachian Mountain Community* (Ph.D. diss., Duke University).

Brown, James S., 1952. *The Family Group in a Kentucky Mountain Farming Community*, University of Kentucky Agricultural Experiment Station Bulletin 588 (Lexington: University of Kentucky Press).

Bryant, F. Carlene, 1979. *We're All Kin: A Cultural Study of an East Tennessee Mountain Neighborhood* (Ph.D. diss., Cornell University).

Campbell, John C., 1921. *The Southern Highlander and His Homeland* (New York: Russell Sage Foundation).

Dominguez, Virginia, 1977. Social Classification in Creole Louisiana. *American Ethnologist* 4:589–602.

Erikson, Kai, 1976. *Everything in Its Path* (New York: Simon and Schuster).

Heller, Peter L., and Gustavo Quesada, 1977. Rural Familism: An Interregional Analysis. *Rural Sociology* 42:220–40.

Hicks, George L., 1976. *Appalachian Valley* (New York: Holt, Rinehart, and Winston).

Jones, Loyal, 1975. Appalachian Values. In *Voices from the Hills*, Robert Higgs and Ambrose Manning, eds. (New York: Frederick Ungar), pp. 507–17.

Kephart, Horace, 1922. *Our Southern Highlanders* (New York: Macmillan).

Leach, Edmund, 1954. *Political Systems of Highland Burma* (Cambridge: Harvard University Press).

Lewis, Helen, Sue Kobak, and Linda Johnson, 1978. Family, Religion, and Colonialism in Central Appalachia. In *Colonialism in Modern America: The Appalachian*

Case, Helen Lewis, Linda Johnson, and Don Askins, eds. (Boone, N.C.: Appalachian Consortium Press), pp. 113–39.

Matthews, Elmore M., 1965. *Neighbor and Kin* (Nashville: Vanderbilt University Press).

Sahlins, Marshall, 1961. The Segmentary Lineage System: An Organization of Predatory Expansion. *American Anthropologist* 63:322–45.

Stack, Carol B., 1974. *All Our Kin: Strategies for Survival in a Black Community* (New York: Harper and Row).

Wallerstein, Immanuel, 1974. *The Modern World-System* (New York: Academic Press).

Walls, David, 1978. Internal Colony or Internal Periphery? A Critique of Current Models and an Alternative Formulation. In *Colonialism in Modern America: The Appalachian Case*, Helen Lewis, Linda Johnson, and Don Askins, eds. (Boone, N.C.: Appalachian Consortium Press), pp. 319–49.

Wolf, Eric, 1966. *Peasants* (Englewood Cliffs, N.J.: Prentice-Hall).

Black Leadership Patterns and Political Change in the American South

YVONNE V. JONES

Traditionally denied access to the formal and informal political arena, black Southerners have utilized a patronage system to influence public policy. Initially, this process involved two groups—influential white patrons and black brokers (or middlemen) who functioned as conduits to both blacks and whites. As a result of federal and state legislation initiated in the 1960s, a third group, black entrepreneurs, operating somewhat autonomously of the traditional patronage system, has emerged. This analysis of two contrasting, but not necessarily competitive, styles of black leadership in a small, rural Piedmont North Carolina community illustrates how changes in the legal status of blacks have acted to reduce their dependency on the local political arena.

The first half of this work describes traditional patterns of black-white articulation. An ecological approach has been utilized to correlate potential leadership roles among blacks with their occupational position within the society as a whole. It will be seen that the ecological arrangements of the community place some blacks in a close structural position to whites of power and position. The second half of the paper focuses on the emergence of black entrepreneurs and compares their role with that of white patrons and traditional black brokers.[1]

Montgomery County,[2] the focus of this study, is a small, predominantly rural community of some 30,000 residents, one-third of whom are black, located on the fringe of the Piedmont region of North Carolina. The county is adjacent to one of the major metropolitan areas of the state and is dotted by mill industries that provide supplemental incomes to farmers, small service stations and grocery stores located at crossroads, and pockets of middle-class housing clusters, or "bedroom communities," whose residents have been attracted to the county by low property taxes and housing prices, and whose interaction with the indigenous residents of the county is minimal. The county has two urban areas, although neither has a population over 4,000. While in the past most of the county's residents secured employment through farm-related activities and mill occupations, many residents are increasingly taking advantage of a wider range of occupations in the metropolitan areas adjacent to the county.

Despite changes in the jural status of blacks enacted by the federal government in the late 1960s (public accommodation laws, voting rights), it was not until the presidential election of 1972 that blacks in Montgomery County actively participated in the state and federal electoral process. Blacks ran unsuccessfully in both the primary and general elections for seats on the county's school board and commission. The current high level of voter participation is, to some extent, a result of changes in the selection process of county and state primary delegates. These changes facilitated participation of a cross-section of the community, thereby diminishing the importance of the local "courthouse gang," a term applied to high status whites who had secured a monopoly on the political positions of importance. Additionally, political volunteers from urban areas adjacent to the county conducted voter registration drives, and local black ministers and farmers encouraged registration and requested political candidates to speak before black audiences. Although blacks at present hold no elected positions in the county government, several have been appointed to citizen commissions, and a few have secured employment in the county government. The all-black county credit union, as well as the Farmers Home Administration, have assumed a more overt political posture, sponsoring forums and scheduling policy-monitoring systems. The addition of federally sponsored community action agencies has increased the range of support services available to blacks and has acted as an organizing vehicle, mobilizing political support when necessary. School integration did not begin until 1972 and took place with a minimum of conflict.

Despite the increased participation by blacks in the public sector, blacks and whites form separate cultural communities and have separate religious and social institutions. There are de facto segregated seating patterns at public forums such as courtrooms and political meetings, and the youth of each ethnic group have separate social functions and claim separate territories or street corners within the county seat. Actions of the county government have often encouraged this schism between black and white youths. In one instance, for example, the town council revoked the permit of a game room frequented by both black and white youths, explaining that the composition of its clientele precipitated complaints from nearby white residents. The labeling of practically all public activities and public places as "belonging" to either ethnic group is most visible in the recently organized federal and state social service organizations. The medical clinic, which consisted of an all-white medical and administrative staff, was defined as a "white" organization despite its integrated clientele and black community outreach workers. Social service organizations, offering a variety of recreational and educational programs to an all-black clientele and administered by an all-black staff, were identified as "belonging" to the black ethnic group.

Interactional patterns are also reinforced by each group's perception of itself, and its place within the historical tradition of the county. Studies of black-white relations in the American South have shown the importance of both internal and external dimensions of ethnic group solidarity. This solidarity reflects the ranking of each group within the hierarchical structure of the county. The feelings of dominance and superiority characteristic of the white ethnic group cited by Powdermaker (1939) and by Davis and Gardner (1941) have been reinforced by codes of racial etiquette and jural regulations that determined segregational patterns based on race. Additionally, the strong emphasis placed on kinship affiliation as a labeling device and as a determination of social status by both blacks and whites acts to intensify the boundaries separating each group. Here, the predominant behavioral norm is racially endogamous marriage practices; segregation of social activities can therefore be seen, in part, as an extension of marital rules.

Although the majority of the county's black residents reside in rural areas, subsisting primarily through farming and mill work, a significant percentage resides in the towns. For the most part, these town blacks have a higher level of education than rural blacks, and their occupations tend to be those associated with urban living. Most town blacks are schoolteachers, shopkeepers, clerks and bookkeepers, truck drivers, and mill workers. One informant labeled these blacks as those who "had to move to town to secure a living," implying that their education had prepared them for nonagricultural occupations. Before school integration, black high schools were located in the towns, even though they primarily served blacks in rural areas. Most of the black school personnel resided near their places of work.

To a large extent, these perceptual, interactional, and residential patterns are an extension of practices formed during the slave era. At best, a system of paternalism existed, in which blacks exchanged their free labor for food, clothing, and shelter—no matter how minimal—and the possibility of protection against the often capricious and violent behavior of some whites. Similarly, the economic activities of the county, especially those which are agriculturally based, can be viewed in this context.

Although slaveholding in Montgomery County during the pre–Civil War period was not extensive, the paternalistic system operative in the antebellum period has continued to evolve in the mid-twentieth century. Presently, there are some rural white and black farmers with long-term economic relationships; the black may be the white's former or present tenant, sharecropper, or domestic worker. Many black farmers lease land from whites during periods of the growing season for the planting of specific crops. This procedure is more complicated than one might expect, for the US Department of Agriculture allows only certain sections of land to be reserved for the growing of specific crops. A black farmer who wishes to plant tobacco, for example, would have to first determine which farm acreage had been assigned a tobacco allotment and then obtain the acreage from the particular white who offered the best deal.[3]

Several changes in these paternalistic dyads are observable. Farmers of both races frequently borrow or exchange farm implements and purchase produce and farm animals from each other. Occasionally black farmers have employed white farmhands, although in most instances these whites are drifters—nonindigenous whites with no ties of kinship in the area who do short-term jobs and then move on—or members of young communal "families" from urban backgrounds who have decided to alter their life-style.

Often local whites and blacks will enter into contractual arrangements where no monies are exchanged (Foster 1967). For example, one black woman agreed to baby-sit for a specified time in return for the repair of her car by a white farmer. Black and white farmers will also harvest each other's crops and assist each other in various other farm projects. Relationships such as these are selective. They are entered into only when blacks, after having carefully evaluated both the nature of the contract and the white personnel involved, determine that the end result will be advantageous to them.

There is some evidence that the particular relationships described above are relatively recent—not more than twenty years old. Elderly black farmers frequently commented on such arrangements as illustrative of the positive change that has recently occurred in race relations. Several factors have encouraged mutually beneficial economic relationships between blacks and whites. The demise of sharecropping in the county has forced many white farmers to enter into different contractual arrangements with blacks in order to continue to maximize their agricultural production. Secondly, a shortage of farm labor in the county today affects both black and white farmers. Finally, the acreage per farm is small, so most farmers find it advantageous to share farm equipment rather than purchase their own.

Relationships between black and white farmers are symbiotic in structure and primarily economic in arrangement. The dyads are selective, involving either the continuation of relationships established with white families in the past or the inception of new relationships with different white families. In either case, the whites must have established a reputation of being fair in their dealings with blacks. If the relationships result in negative repercussions, knowledge of this becomes a part of the evaluative framework used by blacks to assess the potential of future contractual arrangements.

Although these can be thought of primarily as economic relationships, the social aspects are also important. A successful arrangement results in blacks being judged in a favorable light by whites. Furthermore, the borrowing of household articles, the giving of preserves and other foodstuffs, as well as the giving of assistance in times of crisis, are the outgrowths of relationships initially entered into for economic reasons. The result is a social system that is complementary for both groups and mutually adaptive in an environment in which few whites or blacks have large financial reserves.

Whites residing in the towns are primarily shopkeepers, with a scattering of professionals—teachers, doctors, dentists, lawyers, and bankers, as well as such supporting personnel as secretaries and clerical help. Many of the latter reside in rural areas or have kin residing in these areas. What distinguishes them from their rural counterparts is the fact that they have urban occupations and are therefore in a position to form relationships with blacks, who are, in turn, of a different type. Whites residing in the towns, in addition to being the potential dispensers of credit, are the potential dispensers of power.

Relationships between town whites and rural blacks are primarily economic, blacks in many instances being domestic workers of the farmer in either a part- or full-time capacity. Although this master-servant relationship has now almost disappeared (few whites hire domestic workers of any type), relationships between whites who were former masters or mistresses and blacks who were former servants still persist. Their relationships are most obvious during Christmas time and at other holiday occasions. During my stay in the area, for example, several whites brought gifts to elderly blacks residing in rural areas during the Christmas season. These gifts are said to be tokens of appreciation and esteem; it is interesting, although hardly surprising, that blacks were not expected to give gifts in return. These relationships often extend through several generations. For example, the grandson of one former servant was able to enter college because the son-in-law of the former employer interceded on his behalf.

Additionally, blacks residing in rural areas often are able to form relationships with white tradesmen residing in the towns. Again, the relationships are imbedded in an historical continuum similar to the one described for black and white farmers. These relationships are selective, as blacks are most likely to trade at stores where they can receive credit in times of need and where they are treated with courtesy and respect.

This selective bargaining process results in black families' trading at a certain store over the course of several generations. This trend continues despite the construction of several new supermarket chain stores whose prices are often lower. The newly constructed stores provide services based upon efficiency and are impersonal. Although patronizing these stores may provide the buyer with lower prices for high-quality merchandise, the personal relationship between store owner and consumer is absent.

The reputation of the white owner in his dealings with blacks outside the store as well as within his role as store proprietor is an important factor in blacks' decisions whether or not to patronize particular stores. Store owners who are known or suspected to have committed crimes against the black community or to have negative feelings towards blacks are termed "rebish" by the black community and are avoided whenever possible.[4]

Blacks, in turn, are able to establish credit and otherwise capitalize upon their own positive reputations in the eyes of whites. This relationship between rural blacks and white store owners did not become apparent to me until I attempted to purchase some car tires. I was concerned about obtaining the best deal and warranty, and many blacks whom I asked for advice steered me towards a tradesman with whom they had established a personal relationship. It soon became obvious that they wanted these store owners to know that they were instrumental in referring customers to them.

Blacks in rural areas are often able to reciprocate the favors obtained from whites residing in the towns. For example, blacks extend invitations to whites to hunt and fish on their land and often even offer to serve as guides for their guests. Many whites are quick to take advantage of this hospitality, thus extending the relationship beyond the economic sphere. Blacks are thereby able to reinforce the relationship inherent in the patronage system.

Traditional ethnic arrangements have also resulted in middle-class blacks' being cut off from the dyadic relations so far discussed. This is due primarily to the perception by many whites that these blacks had broken an unwritten code of behavior by obtaining an education and were thus attempting to upset ethnic arrangements based upon the superiority of whites and the inferiority of blacks. One should not assume, however, that these middle-class blacks, who reside largely in the towns, are totally outside the range of the dyadic relations already discussed. Because blacks residing in the towns are the off-shoots of rural kin clusters, they are able to utilize the established ties of their rural kinsmen, with the rural kinsmen acting as intermediaries between those whites with whom they have established relationships and their town-dwelling kinsmen. When one black woman wanted to be considered for a position as a teacher's aide, for example, she asked a rural kinsman to intercede on her behalf. The rural kinsman had established a brokerage relationship with someone on the school board to whom he delivered wood.

Not all blacks residing in towns have rural kin, however. A few others are able to present requests and obtain favors directly from whites, but these are generally those blacks in occupations that (1) involve frequent contact with whites and (2) are subordinate to the positions of the whites from whom they are trying to obtain a favor. Until recently, initiating such relationships involved gaining acceptance from individual whites; continuing the relationship depended upon maintaining a behavioral code that showed deference to the status of the white, or family of whites, whom one wanted to retain as a potential patron. The great majority of town whites with whom blacks have maintained a patronage relationship are those who have status and power within the white community. Blacks who can be considered "professional" are those blacks who have purposely refused to participate in the behavioral rituals that require members of the subordinate ethnic group to show deference and respect.

To summarize, the relationships between blacks and whites in Montgomery County represent an extension of paternalistic ties first developed during the slave era. Rural black and white farmers frequently assist each other in agricultural activities and in times of crisis, as well as borrow household articles and farm implements. Rural black farmers have primarily economic relationships with town whites who are perceived to be liberal and fair in their dealings with the blacks. Town blacks, clustered in nonagricultural occupations and often regarded as "uppity," frequently utilize rural kinsmen to intercede on their behalf.

Although articulation between many blacks and whites is primarily economic, some blacks are aware of the potential favors which can result from such a relationship. They can utilize these relationships to benefit themselves or their families, or they can use them to benefit the black community as a whole.

As the legal status of blacks began to change in the 1960s, some traditional brokers, like Samuel Walden, were formally incorporated into official political bodies, albeit in appointed rather than elected positions. Early in his life, Walden, now in his late seventies, obtained a favorable relationship with several influential whites which allowed him to be instrumental in establishing several black organizations, the most significant of which were an all-black credit union and a Farmers Home Administration. Today Mr. Walden serves as a member of the police advisory board of the county seat and on several other organizations that previously consisted of white members only. Another individual, Leah Dean, an elderly black woman, was able to utilize her considerable influence among county officials to enable me to gain access to county records. Like Samuel Walden, she was instrumental in organizing the black Farmers Home Administration and credit union more than thirty years ago, and hence has a history of dealing with whites to accomplish certain ends. Their status vis-à-vis the white community has become "official" in that both are now called upon to act as spokespersons and representatives of county blacks on various local governmental bodies. Although they have held the position of "broker" for some time, recent state and federal enactments requiring black representation on formerly all-white citizen advisory commissions have sanctioned their brokerage roles among both blacks and whites.

Not all black brokers are elderly or in farm-related occupations. Many younger local black residents have recently entered occupations comparable to those held by whites. Their entry into these previously closed positions is due to both federal and state equal opportunity and affirmative action programs. Their presence has acted to expand the number of resources that can be utilized in times of crisis or to circumvent racist practices of some whites.

One example of this is the role played by a black bank teller hired by one of the largest banks in the county seat. After observing her actions over a long period, it became clear to me that many black as well as white bank customers thought that her primary role was to serve black customers. But she is the only teller who sells food stamps, utilized primarily by blacks. Most of the customers she serves are black, and they will stand in line to be waited on by her even when the other bank tellers are not busy. In addition to her role as a teller, she is often observed using her position to facilitate other bank transactions of black customers. On one occasion, a black man attempted to get a check cashed by a white teller. He was unable to do so, left the building, and told another black of his problem. The person he approached called the bank teller and requested that she cash the check, which she did. In the absence of a black bank teller, the task would have been performed either through a white intermediary or not at all.

The black assistant principal of a formerly all-white high school plays a similar role. This person had occupied an administrative position in the old black high school. After the integration of the public school system, he became assistant principal and is presently the only black to occupy such a high position in this integrated school. Because of his position in the administrative system, he is called upon to act as an intermediary by black students and by concerned parents when they are having a problem with white school personnel. He has been instrumental in preventing the expulsion of several black students and in one instance was able to prevent a school boycott by students.

The boycott was threatened in response to student rumors that the white principal had verbally abused a black female student, calling her a "nigger" among other derogatory terms. Some black students who learned of the incident threatened to boycott classes. The principal then asked to meet with the students in the presence of the black assistant principal. The assistant principal was able to convince the students to postpone their boycott and attend the meeting. The issue was eventually settled, the black assistant principal having played a significant role in the resolution of this conflict.

There is a considerable awareness of the value of these brokers among whites, so that in times of potential racial violence, black brokers often act as intermediaries between figures of authority and members of both ethnic groups. Let me cite an example. The principal of the high school published a new handbook of rules and regulations for the school. It stressed, among other things, proper attire and behavior both during school hours and at school events after hours. The principal requested that the parents sign statements indicating that they had read the handbook and would accept responsibility if their children violated the rules; students were told that they would be suspended if the statements were not signed. One black mother protested the harsh and threatening tone of the statement, stressing that signing the notice was equal to signing a contract in order to allow her child to attend school—a violation of the laws governing public school attendance. She brought up her objections to the handbook at an open board of education meeting from which the principal of the high school was absent; his absence curtailed full discussion until a later meeting.

In the interim, one county newspaper picked up the item and reported on it in its weekly issue, while another newspaper presented an evaluation of the rules published in the handbook and commented that some of the rules discriminated against black students. Both the ethnic identity of the parent and the newspaper's assessment of the handbook was enough to publicly signal the incident as a black issue.

When the school board met again, it became apparent that the black assistant principal was there to minimize the demands and objections of the protesting parent and of other blacks who were present. At frequent intervals the white principal looked for verbal confirmation from the black assistant principal, who found himself in a rather awkward situation—he was serving as a broker for two groups of people at the same time. As one black informant later told me, "He was in a fix. He had to go home to his wife after the meeting, and appear at the schoolhouse door the next morning."

Black brokers encompass a range of occupations and ages. Older brokers have held their positions longer and have established an ongoing relationship with white patrons. Older brokers take a more public stance and are perceived by both blacks and whites as political leaders. Their service on a variety of civic organizations within the black community and their appointment to local governmental boards and commissions have reinforced this image. Younger black brokers, by contrast, assume a less public position and serve primarily to facilitate transactions between black customers and white institutions. Both brokers, however, are old residents of the county and are closely tied to its economic structure. This restricts their independence and minimizes the degree of political autonomy that they have in relation to the all-white political structure.

Unlike brokers, whose political power and stature is dependent upon the cultivation of persons and/or networks that are directly or indirectly involved in political decisionmaking, black entrepreneurs in Montgomery County have access to resources similar to those available to white patrons. These entrepreneurs are generally young and well educated. More important, these blacks do not reside in the county and are not related by kinship to county folks. Their presence in the area is due to the emergence of federally supported social service agencies, which are actually rural extensions—in terms of administration and management—of social service organizations located in the surrounding metropolitan areas outside the county. Since these programs derive their support from state and federal sources, they are fiscally independent of the local political system. Although designed to serve both white and black clientele, these agencies have a primarily black clientele, and consequently, an image within the county as black programs.

These black entrepreneurs have considerable resources at their disposal. The agencies provide emergency housing and food assistance, supplemental educational programs for youths and adults, and organized recreational activities. They conduct voter education programs, a social service program for the elderly, and a transportation program for the predominately rural county. These black entrepreneurs also facilitate transactions between local blacks and resources located outside of the county. They have a thorough knowledge of scholarship programs and employment training programs, and they use the extensive networks of their organizations to secure employment and training positions outside the county. They also offer legal guidance in problems which arise during the probation of wills, property tax assessments, and land disputes. Since there are no black attorneys in the county, in the past blacks used white attorneys to resolve their legal problems. While it was felt that these local attorneys did not properly represent their black clients' interests, considerable use was made of black brokers who had attorneys as patrons. The presence of black entrepreneurs who themselves have no formal legal training but know of black attorneys or law firms that specialize in property law or civil litigation has diminished the power of local white attorneys. In fact, local attorneys frequently complain that the social service personnel of these agencies are, in effect, practicing law without a license; these attorneys even make personal visits to the homes of blacks who had been clients in the past in order to retain their services.

While their function is not overtly political, these entrepreneurs do provide local residents with the information necessary to challenge the activities of the county government system. In one instance, the county commissioners decided to decline the offer of community development funds, citing increased paperwork and outside federal interference as reasons for their decision. But federal guidelines require public discussion and consensus before funds can be accepted or rejected and before the use of such funds can be determined. When the black entrepreneurs informed blacks of the recently enacted open meeting laws, as well as the regulations pertaining to community development funds, the county commissioners were forced to rescind their earlier decision and to hold a series of meetings throughout the county attended by a large percentage of blacks. Eventually, the commissioners decided to accept the federal monies.

In contrast to the high visibility of black brokers in the political arena, black entrepreneurs assume a low political posture. They do not attend meetings of the town council or county commissioners, nor do they articulate with the local Democratic party structure. Lack of residency within the county prevents them from running for political office or being appointed to a local board or government task force. They have not sought to establish long-term relations with politically influential whites. Concurrently, these entrepreneurs provide considerable resources and assistance to local black voluntary organizations and churches, and often participate in their activities. They are familiar figures at weekend church homecomings and family reunions, often attending these events with their spouses and children. This dual strategy results in these nonindigenous black entrepreneurs' achieving a high level of acceptance among local blacks, and minimizes their being placed in a competitive position with indigenous black brokers.

The success of black entrepreneurs is due to the degree of independence they have been able to achieve in not utilizing the local system of white patronage. The function of these federally supported social service organizations is not dependent upon local white approval, nor are their personnel dependent upon local fiscal policies. Essentially, entrepreneurs dispense the services of the federal government and utilize their knowledge of governmental procedure to check the actions of local political structures. This acts to reduce the level of dependency of black residents upon the local political system and to expand their network of resources and knowledge beyond county boundaries.

Despite their functions, entrepreneurs should be viewed as having transitional roles. As federal support for social service programs of this type diminishes, local fiscal support will become necessary. Envisioning such a possibility, these entrepreneurs have sought to establish long-term relations with local whites by utilizing the following techniques: (1) employing local whites of low-income status who have historically lacked patronage contacts with local whites of power; (2) cultivating an image of concern for those of low income regardless of race; and (3) instituting recreational programs in areas of the county that are predominately white. By expanding their services to include whites, these entrepreneurs are hopeful that their image as administrators of "black-only" organizations will diminish and place them in a position to secure local white support. As this support becomes increasingly necessary, their political strategies will change, as will their relationship with the county political system.

The role of entrepreneurs and brokers is in large measure a reflection of federal and state enactments that compel local communities to include blacks in the local decisionmaking process. Brokers, the former clients of white patrons, are long-term residents of the county who have built up a reputation among local whites with moderate views on social equality. These brokers, the majority of whom are over sixty, are generally thought to be "Uncle

Toms" by younger blacks, but are usually successful in obtaining social and political change because of their historical ties with white patrons who serve on local bank boards and school commissions or are presently town or county commissioners.[5]

Their role contrasts sharply with that of the entrepreneurs, who may or may not reside in the county and whose power rests in their ability to utilize a professional or occupational network extending beyond the county to various federal and state agencies that monitor the compliance of local communities with the various civil rights acts. Because a large percentage of the operating funds of these agencies is obtained from federal and state budgets, the employment of these entrepreneurs does not depend upon the favoritism of the local community. They provide a service to blacks by offering employment that is not dependent upon county whites and by monitoring the activities of the all-white formal political system (Jones 1975).

Taken as a whole, the services of both types complement each other. The first type is utilized by blacks almost exclusively to obtain jobs and to support certain programs beneficial to blacks within the county. For example, a black wishing to run for a county government post or to secure employment within the county government system can use black brokers who were the former clients of the white community. Blacks seeking employment that is not dependent upon county whites or petitioning against decisions in employment or local tax disputes can utilize the entrepreneurs who are the directors of community action agencies or public health centers. Although many of the problems these entrepreneurs are asked to resolve do not fall under the auspices of the agencies that they direct, they are frequently able to put blacks in touch with appropriate state or federal agencies. Furthermore, these agencies often can provide needed services for the county: health services, tutoring of school children, emergency funds, and social programs.

Whereas patron-client and colleague relationships are frequently most beneficial to particular black families, entrepreneurs are placed in positions that tend to benefit the entire black community. These positions are the result of the shifting ethnic boundaries which have come about within the county largely because of federal intervention in the civil rights arena. Whereas blacks previously depended upon the internal power structure of the county to secure social, economic, and political favors, they can now look to black brokers and entrepreneurs to provide a more comprehensive alternative. To a large degree, the power of both broker and entrepreneur rests in the fact that they are economically independent of the county, being either retired or directors of state and federal social service problems.

The present biracial character of Montgomery County embodies multiple relationships based upon the complementary nature of the groups with respect to some of their cultural features. This articulation occurs within the context of cultural rules in which both blacks and whites assign symbolic meanings to certain types of ethnic interaction. The implementation of the various strategies mentioned in this paper is dependent upon the important features of status and role as they operate within the white community and the ability of the blacks to be cognizant of this. Rather than viewing the social order as a static, polarized biracial system, the argument presented here is that, while some types of interethnic articulation correspond to the integrative elements within the culture and allow for some type of equilibrium to take place in Montgomery County, the demands of blacks that do not fit into traditionally held notions of black-white relationships are filtered through black entrepreneurs who employ nonlocal agencies and personnel to check the restrictions of the county's white political system. The strategies undertaken by these newly ascribed black entrepreneurs are in many instances in conflict with local norms. The result is a competitive, dynamic situation in which white patrons try to maintain power, elderly black brokers seek to continue their dual positions, and newly ascribed young black entrepreneurs seek to shift the boundaries of traditional ethnic articulation.

NOTES

Fieldwork was undertaken during the summer of 1972 through a small grant from the University of North Carolina, Chapel Hill; from July 1974 through August 1975, with the support of a Dissertation Fellowship from the American Association of University Women, and for a shorter period during the summer of 1976. I wish to thank John Bodine, Lynn Burkhart, Julia Crane, Fredrick Hicks, Carole Hill, Ruth Landman, and James Peacock for their many helpful comments on an earlier draft of this paper.

1. Boissevian (1974) has distinguished between two types of brokerage patterns. While both brokers and entrepreneurs act as conduits to third parties, the strategies undertaken by entrepreneurs are more likely to involve a high degree of risk and employ nontraditional and innovative techniques. Hence, entrepreneurs operate outside of the fringe of established communication channels, while brokers use more conservative strategies.

2. A pseudonym.

3. There are no sharecroppers in the county. The leasing arrangement referred to in these instances involves farmers who periodically rent additional acreage for specific purposes. This arrangement shows up in the US Department of Agriculture census under "renters."

4. "Rebish" is a term blacks apply to those whites whose behavior is thought to be hostile to blacks, who are thought to belong to the Ku Klux Klan, or who are from certain sections of the South that have a reputation of being especially harsh to blacks.

5. As of November 1976, there were no black elected officials in the county.

REFERENCES

Boissevian, Jeremy, 1974. *Friends of Friends: Networks, Manipulators, and Coalitions* (New York: St. Martin's Press).

Davis, Allison, and Burleigh B. Gardner, 1941. *Deep South* (Chicago: University of Chicago Press).

Foster, George M., 1967. The Dyadic Contract: A Model for the Social Structure of a Mexican Peasant Village. In *Peasant Society: A Reader*, May Diaz and George Foster, eds. (Boston: Little, Brown), pp. 213–29.

Jones, Yvonne V., 1975. *Ethnicity and Political Process in a Southern Rural Community: An Examination of Black-White Articulation in Decision-Making* (Ph.D. diss., American University).

Powdermaker, Hortense, 1939. *After Freedom: A Cultural Study in the Deep South* (New York: Viking).

Fortress without Walls:
A Black Community after Slavery

SYDNEY NATHANS

This inquiry started with a single document. It was a slave register and had on it 109 names of men, women, and children who in 1844 were sent from one of the largest estates in North Carolina to a newly purchased cotton plantation in Alabama. Both plantations belonged to Paul Cameron, North Carolina's largest slaveholder and wealthiest man by 1860. Famous in its time, the North Carolina plantation has become for historians a unique source of study, because the owners' century-long correspondence and records—as well as their homes, outbuildings, and slave quarters—have been preserved.[1] Paul Cameron's Alabama land had a different fate. Sold off in parcels after 1870, the land and the community of people on it "disappeared" from the historical record. In 1978, I asked myself, Is it possible to locate that land, to find the descendants of the people sent to it, and above all, to recover the story of that community of black immigrants in slavery and freedom? I began with the list of 109 people, almost all identified by first names only. After a summer of research in North Carolina and Alabama I determined the exact location of the old plantation, in Hale County, Alabama, discovered the church and school that the black freedmen had established on it, and found descendants rich with memory of their history from the time of the 1844 migration down to the present. A remarkable story began to unfold.

It was soon evident that the black community in Alabama was marked by notable continuity. One of the few last names given in the original Cameron slave register of 1844 was also listed in the local telephone directory and carved on the cornerstone in front of the community church. Names of individuals residing in the locality in the 1870s—names found in the deed books and mortgage records and in the 1870 manuscript census—were also painted on mailboxes throughout the settlement. The church and the school, mentioned in a letter from the overseer to the plantation owner in 1872, stood in almost the same spot described by the overseer a century before. Here were descendants of families forced to migrate to Alabama in slavery times who had fashioned a community for themselves and held onto it for more than a century. How had they done it? What kind of world had they created?

Land and religion, it became clear, were central to the maintenance of this black settlement over time. Paul Cameron had sold his Alabama plantation to black people. "All black, no white," was how one descendant put it, and with one exception the names in the deed record books bore her out: all black, no white. Cameron had sold off his land to blacks who had put no money down and paid off their debt in bales of cotton over a five-year period. By 1884, each of the black landowners on this plantation possessed considerably more than "forty acres and a mule." Most had more than a hundred acres, and owned mules, oxen, and cattle to boot.[2]

Yet if land provided the economic wherewithal for individuals, religion provided spiritual resources that were essential to the coherence of the community for more than a century. The complementary role of land and religion can be suggested by brief encapsulations of the experiences of members of three generations in the settlement's history since emancipation. For the first generation, the focus is on Paul Hargress, a former slave who obtained land and made it the basis of several family business partnerships. For the second generation, attention shifts to Forrest Hargress, who dedicated much of his life to sustaining a religious community in the settlement. For the third generation, the inquiry turns to the experience of individuals who left and returned to the community in the twentieth century, and explores the function of the settlement in a time of massive out-migration.

Carrie Davis was a child when she knew Paul Hargress early in the twentieth century. She recalls him as "a huge of a man," with a thick, long gray moustache that curved down on each side toward his shoulders. He had a "high, fine voice." And that voice often told of how it was when he came out to Alabama as a slave. The other slaves, he often repeated, walked their way out from North Carolina, perhaps linked by a chain. Not Paul Hargress. He came out on a coach with Paul Cameron himself. Together they crossed the Blue Ridge Mountains, separate from the rest of the work force. When Cameron left Paul Hargress behind on his Alabama plantation, he gave Paul Hargress a small bag of gold.[3] There is no corroboration for the story. But what the story seemed to suggest was fascinating: that Paul Hargress viewed himself as a trusted man, a cut above the others, a man who saw himself as much a partner of the master as his slave.

When freedom came, Paul, his brother Jim, and at least four other former slaves took the name Hargress—the name of the family they had belonged to before the Camerons obtained title to them sometime in the 1830s. Along with another group of Cameron's former slaves who took the name Cameron—which for some later became Cannon—the family groups continued to live on and work the plantation.[4] After a tempestuous three years from 1865 to 1868, in which the freedmen signaled in various ways that they felt claims on the land, displayed a strong interest in the assertions of radical Republican politicians that they *deserved* the land, and made it clear that *they* would decide how much labor their families would contribute to work on the plantation, they seemed to reach a modus vivendi with the beleaguered overseer, who had managed the plantation continuously since 1859.[5]

In 1868, Paul and Jim Hargress and Sandy Cameron became supervisors of three squads of laborers who worked the plantation and brought the land they plowed back to prewar levels of productivity. Freedmen elsewhere in Alabama and the South often rebelled against working the land in a manner so reminiscent of slavery days. Perhaps the postwar role was made easier for the three squad leaders by the probability that they had been slave drivers before emancipation.[6] Despite the best effort of the labor force, the plantation did not flourish. Poor weather and worms, not poor labor, cut down the cotton crop of 1868. The prior departure from the estate of perhaps the bulk of the labor force meant that broomsedge began to encroach on the uncultivated portion of the plantation, giving the land an unkempt look to neighbors.[7] The repeated poor crops and reports of continued political instability led Paul Cameron to consider by 1870 the sale of his land.

As numerous historians have discerned from the written record, many former slaves chose after freedom to stay on or near the homeplace. On Cameron's Alabama land, as on other plantations, ties of kin and community were of major importance in that decision. The clearest evidence of a commitment to continue the community begun in slavery came in 1872, when white overseer Wilson O'Berry suggested to Paul Cameron that they set aside an acre of land for the creation of a church and a school. The savvy overseer gave his reasons: "I want to know if you will let me have one acre of land. . . . it is for the Purpus of building of a negroe church also for a school house. It will be a neighborhood busyness and you will see my reasons for it. It is to manage to ceep [*sic*] hands in the neighborhood. In the neighborhood where farmers have done this they invarybly can get a plenty of hands." But in the final sentence of his letter he revealed that the idea and the initiative for the school and the church had come from the black families on the plantation: "They will pay for it [in] cash."[8] Cameron did not accept the offer, deciding instead to try to sell off his land. But families constructed a brush-arbor church on the acre anyhow, on the very spot designated in the overseer's letter.

Paul and Jim Hargress were able to buy 120 acres of Paul Cameron's land in the mid-1870s, and a family partnership began. Paul, Jim, and Squire Hargress, along with other members of the family, worked the land. They used the crops, the tools, the farm animals, and the land itself as the basis for cash advances from local merchants. The mortgage deed records show that for a time they prospered. Without children of his own, Paul needed farm laborers. Without land, Paul's brother-in-law's family and Paul's other relatives needed a place to work. A family partnership evolved.[9]

No evidence indicates that Paul Hargress, like Nate Shaw in Theodore Rosengarten's *All God's Dangers* (1974), sought to use his land or his family for "striving," for getting ahead. For him, for Sandy Cameron, and for others in the first generation of freedom, all effort seemed directed instead at getting and holding onto their foothold in the Alabama earth. The goal of "getting by," to use a phrase I heard numerous times in interviews, will come as no surprise to students of post-plantation and peasant societies. Paul Hargress never bought any land in addition to his purchase of the 1870s; his quantity of mules and tools and credit remained stable from year to year. Security and independence seemed to be what he sought and what hard labor wrested for him.

Independence and security for Paul Hargress became harder to maintain in the twentieth century. Widowed, aging, and childless at the turn of the century, this "huge of a man" nonetheless might have continued to make his land pay had he not been "cut down" one night in the early 1900s. An ice storm froze Hale County. Paul Hargress's poorly insulated cabin, with openings in the roof and with crevices in the floor big enough for a quarter to drop through, did not hold what heat there was. His leg froze and had to be amputated. Two in the community who were not blood-kin "adopted" "Unc Paul" and looked after him. He seemed to resent the fact that those closer to him by bloodline showed insufficient concern. "Family? I don't know any family!" he once despaired angrily.[10] But he did have blood-kin close by, and one last time linked their interest with his land in a family business partnership. He deeded off his land in eleven equal parcels to his nine blood-kin and the two "adopted" kin who cared for him, contingent on their agreeing to pay him ten dollars cash each October and agreeing further to pay one-eleventh each of his burial costs and his outstanding debts upon his death.[11] Paul Hargress thus contracted with his kin for them to provide his pension and his burial insurance. They—many farm laborers living and working on nearby estates— moved onto "Unc Paul's" land and built cabins there. Unc Paul's final partnership created for the next generation a measure of independence and security of their own. It was a smaller foothold than Paul Hargress had possessed. But in the twentieth century, as the life of one of the next generation would reveal, even a small foothold provided a measure of independence and was better than no foothold at all.

The sack of gold? Rumor had it—after Paul Hargress's death in 1918—that he had buried it under the cherry tree in front of his house. People in the community today can still recall hearing the sounds of searchers scraping and digging at night for the buried treasure. The digging went on for weeks—until the cherry tree collapsed into a gaping hole. No one knows if the gold was ever found after Paul Hargress's death. But in his life, the gold had served as an emblem of aspirations for this "huge of a man": partnership, independence, and holding onto what he had.[12]

Ned Forrest Hargress was one of the adopted kin who early in the twentieth century assumed the duties of "son" to Paul Hargress and who looked after Paul Hargress until his death in 1918. In one way Forrest Hargress's background was exceptional. According to family tradition, he was the son of Dorothy, a cook on the Alabama plantation, and of a Confederate officer who had forced himself on her while his troops were encamped near the plantation during the final days of the Civil War.[13] In many other ways, Forrest Hargress's long life—which began in 1866 and ended a century later during the months of civil rights demonstrations in his hometown of Greensboro, Alabama—typified the lives of the black community's second generation in freedom.[14] He married the daughter of a member of the original community, Betty Cameron. He and his wife inherited thirty acres owned by his father-in-law, Sandy Cameron, and he acquired an additional eighteen acres in return for his aid to Paul Hargress.

Ned Forrest Hargress's inheritance—a white father, fifty acres of land—gave him and his family a measure of independence during his lifetime. But neither proved sufficient to permit him complete autonomy, or to support his family of twelve children. Like so many, he had to labor for others—but for others, not under them. Insulted by one employer when he came on a Saturday morning, hat in hand, to ask for some molasses—"Can't you niggers let a man read his newspaper on his porch in peace?"—he could put on his hat and reply, "Cap'n Earl, my daddy was as white as you are!" and stalk away. With enough land for a "house seat" of his own, he could take off a Monday from work when he wanted to, and if challenged by his employer—"Where you goin' with that mule and wagon, Forrest?"—retort, "I'se goin' to town just like you are Cap'n Jim."[15] And he could get away with it. But for income and perhaps also for "influence" with a white patron in the county, he hired out his labor in addition to tending to his own land and crops.

But though his white father and his property-holdings were doubtless factors in Forrest Hargress's independence, when I talked to one resident about this, he brought me up short. I told my source—who had known Hargress for fifty years—that everything I had heard made Forrest Hargress sound like a pretty independent man. "Oh, I don't know that he was so independent. He was a *Christian* man."[16] As I listened more, it became clear that Forrest Hargress did not spend the bulk of his time trying to get along with or rebuff challenges from white folks. Nor did he spend all his energies just trying to make a living or get a bit ahead, though he did go to the field most days and though he did energetically supplement his income by making and selling work-baskets and by running a molasses mill and small candy and grocery store.[17] Much of his energy and effort went into being a Christian and into making his community a *Christian* community.

For Forrest Hargress and for his generation, it was not only land, not only family networks, but the vibrant religious life of the community that gave the settlement its strength and longevity. After 1900, their church was no longer a brush-arbor construction in the woods but a weatherboard building with green shutters on the outside. Inside, it had a large chandelier holding dozens of candles.[18] Members of the community—which included forty to fifty families who worked adjacent lands as tenants, as well as the families of landowners— gathered in church for much of the day on Sunday, into the night every Wednesday, and for a full week at revival time. On all occasions, the church was always described to me as "full to overflowing." Revivals were special occasions, when the congregation swelled with prayers for the unbaptized, who sat on the mourners' bench while others prayed and wept for their souls, until the spirit came and they "confessed religion." When the baptisms oc- curred, it was again a collective event for the entire community. All would come out for the processional through the settlement from the church to the waters of Little Prairie Creek. When a member of the community died or sud- denly took ill, a bell near the church pealed loudly—it was called "toning the bell"—and the entire settlement poured in from the field or out of their homes to learn who had fallen and to give aid. Repeatedly people used the same phrase to describe the sheer density of the people in the settlement and their density on religious occasions especially: "There was so many folks you couldn't stir 'em with a stick." [19] Such stories of the past and the still-intense spirituality of the church service today suggest the presence of a powerful re- ligious culture, a fortress without walls, that over the generations has sus- tained the community's way of life.

Yet there were flourishing elements of culture in the community that were distinctly outside the pale of religion. The community had its own stores, its own baseball team, its own brass bands that played into the night, its own gambling dens. Sacred and secular cultures might contest each other loudly, as when the strains of the brass bands and the parties they announced could be heard mixing with religious singing from a church-sponsored picnic called the "Festival in the Wilderness." Or the sacred and the profane might contest covertly when a church member and family man would hire a "rambling man" to buy a ticket to the church picnic for his "outside woman." [20] In this community, as on the plantation of slavery days and as in the communities of other working people in the nineteenth and early twentieth centuries, the sa- cred, the secular, and the profane, the churched and the unchurched, coexisted in close physical proximity.[21]

In this setting, what did Christian men like Forrest Hargress do? As best they could, they policed the settlement, seeking to maintain a code of moral strictness. If Forrest Hargress came upon a game of craps, the gamblers scattered at the sight of him. If he identified some of the sinners as church members, they were reported. If a church man was overheard to swear "Well, I'll be goddamned"—as one was when he discovered that his unwed daughter had given birth to a child—he lost his membership in the church. Parents were strict with their children, disciplining them heavily and often. And *any* adult in the community was entitled to punish physically the misbehavior of *any* child in the settlement. If the child complained of the whipping to his parents, he got thrashed again at home.[22] Yet along with the code of strictness went leniency, the obligation to forgive, and the mechanisms for redemption. Parents and children were urged to forgive each other their offenses. Those ostracized from church for misbehavior could appear before the preacher or the congregation to "beg pardon," and receive it promptly. Even the men "called to preach"—the holiest calling in the settlement—were expected to "go slack" and need redeeming forgiveness.[23]

How did this mixture of moral strictness and ready forgiveness help maintain the community? The strictness was not just rural black Puritanism. It was not, as H. L. Mencken might have put it, the fear by a righteous few that somewhere, someone in the settlement might be happy. Moral strictness was a means to autonomy. That autonomy was partly spiritual, the peace and strength that comes from walking right with God. But the autonomy was also worldly. As one mother told her children, they had better "*behave*," for she did not have and would not seek "influence" with a white man to save them if they got into trouble.[24] Yet the close proximity of the sacred and profane in the settlement heightened the chances for lapses. The Christian men and women and the church stood ready always to forgive and reclaim the faithful. Moral strictness, forgiveness, and day-to-day generosity helped to cement together the second-generation families of the community. Their qualities were embodied in Forrest Hargress, "a Christian man."

The role of the home settlement for many in the third generation since emancipation has been different from what it was for their forebears. Most have gone out into the world; most of those still in the settlement today have come home again. For many in the third generation, wide-ranging migration became a necessity. The sheer press of people on the land, and natural disasters such as the boll weevil and the flood of 1916, increased pressure to leave. But many were lured away, especially by the increased employment of blacks in industry and in the coal mines of Alabama. For some, migration was the alternative to economic strangulation. For others, it offered an escape from intense family strain or—for a young man—the chance to "ramble" and "to be a man!"[25]

Many of the third generation who inhabit the community today have come

back from the larger world. One couple hastened back from living in Bessemer, Alabama, a mining city, after lightning struck a trolley they were in.
They took it as an omen, and two weeks after their return in 1919 an explosion
in the mine killed dozens of the husband's friends. Another member of the
community, forced during the depression to seek work elsewhere, was cut up
one night in a knife fight. He returned home in 1937 and has spent most of
his time there since, vigorous but bound to a wheelchair. One woman, after
twenty-five years of labor in Detroit and New York, bought herself a bright
red trailer and returned home to "go fishin'." Another woman recalled that
one year she and her husband moved onto a white man's land to "try and get
ahead." All they got was debt, and the next year moved back to stay.[26] The
outside world for many seemed to be the same—high hopes but harsh realities, a devil with a crooked smile and a snaggle-toothed grin.

What does the homeplace mean to those of the third generation who reside
there today? James Lyles is such a man. In striking ways, he embodies the
values of his forbears. Like Paul Hargress, he owns a portion of the original
Alabama plantation and has a deep attachment to it. Like Ned Forrest Hargress, he lacks a "literary education" but is a deeply Christian man and lives
by "the Master Book." Like so many of his own generation, he has migrated
out into the world and returned home from it. James Lyles left first in 1916, a
young man eager to get free of home and to ramble. He worked in the mines,
first in Bessemer, then in West Virginia. He was called back by a premonition,
by a visit from the spirit telling him his mother was ill. He returned; she was;
he stayed. After he married and began a family, he went out a second time to
the mines in the 1930s—the only way, during the Great Depression, that he
could support a large family and keep from losing his homeplace to creditors.
By 1944, he had earned enough to reclaim the land from debt and his sons
were old enough to contribute their labor to the farm. He returned home again
and for good.[27]

James Lyles knows that many young people think differently than he does
about the home settlement. He knows that most are now off to Birmingham
and Detroit and the West Coast. He knows that though they come back tem-
porarily—for family reunions, for church homecomings, sometimes for July
4th or Christmas—many believe they will never return. He knows that some
of the current generation are even ready to sell out their portion of the home
settlement from which they came. He thinks they are wrong. What will happen in the city when people find they cannot eat, or cannot work, and need a
home again?

So James Lyles is holding on to his inheritance, to the sanctuary for three
generations, to what he calls the "plant bed" in which so many seeds have
taken root and flourished. When they need to, James Lyles's children and
grandchildren will have a place to come home again.[28] In holding on to the
land and the Lord, James Lyles carries on a long tradition.

NOTES

1. Herbert Gutman in his *The Black Family in Slavery and Freedom* (1976) and George McDaniel in oral interviews have delineated the genealogies and family relationships of the Bennehan-Cameron black families in North Carolina. The Camerons' North Carolina plantation, Stagville, just north of Durham, is now a state historic site and a Center for the Study of Historical Preservation.

2. Interview with Alice Hargress, August 1978, Hale County, Alabama. Confirmation of the oral testimony came through tracing the sale of the Cameron estate in the deed books of Hale County, which are located in the Office of the Probate Judge, Greensboro, Alabama. Sixteen individuals bought Cameron's land from 1872 to 1889; through other written and oral sources, I have identified fifteen as black. Cameron authorized the sale of his lands through a local lawyer who acted as his agent. Sales commenced in 1872; all but 200 acres were sold by 1885. Cameron tried to sell in tracts ranging from 80 to 240 acres. Only one black landowner, Sandy Cameron, came to own a very small tract. His 30 acres represented all he could hold on to after he failed to meet the payments on the 160 acres he had originally contracted to purchase.

The Cameron correspondence suggests that Cameron first sought a single purchaser for the entire 1,600-acre plantation. No buyer made an adequate offer. Both an Alabama landowner and his son-in-law informed him that the only way to get his price was to sell the land in smaller tracts. Every purchaser paid at least the minimum of $8 per acre that Cameron required; most paid $10 per acre for the land. A. G. Jones (Greensboro) to Paul Cameron, 6 October 1869; George P. Collins to Cameron, 7 December, 11 December, 1869, in Cameron Family Papers, Southern Historical Collection, University of North Carolina (hereafter abbreviated SHC).

3. Interview with Carrie Hargress Davis, August 1979; interviews with Louis Rainey, August 1978 and July 1979.

4. To avoid confusion in the paper, I use here the name Hargress. The name in fact varied over time in the places it was written down. The name first appeared in the 1844 register of slaves sent to Alabama, where "Jim Hargis" was one of several slaves listed with a surname. In the 1866 manuscript census for Alabama, there is a York Hogis listed. The postwar plantation overseer referred in 1868 to Jim and Paul Hargrove. The names in the manuscript census, the deed books, and the mortgage records also vary, from Hargess in the 1880s to Hargress in 1918. It seems probable that Paul and Jim and the other members of the families who took the name Hargis/Hargress derived the name from that of a business partner of Duncan Cameron, who sold or transferred his slaves to Cameron in the 1830s.

5. Wilson O'Berry to Paul Cameron, 11 August 1867, Cameron Family Papers, SHC.

6. O'Berry to Cameron, 6 April 1868, Cameron Family Papers, SHC. In this letter, the overseer reported: "The negroes are working well and have been all of the year, and behave themselves well. I have the best lot of hands in Hale Co. . . . Jim Hargrove is at the head of one squad Paul at the head of another and Wesley at the head of the other one. . . . [Wesley] is a very industrious boy . . . he does not mind whipping them no more than he did in slavery time. Sandy works his 4 hands besides himself and have planted a good crop." The terms of agreement between the overseer and the squad leaders are not revealed in the letters. Because O'Berry rented the entire postwar plantation from Cameron, and then made his own terms with the "hands," he was under no obligation to reveal the labor contract to the owner.

7. O'Berry to Cameron, 17 June, 13 September 1868; George P. Collins (Greensboro) to Cameron, 11 December 1869, Cameron Family Papers, SHC.

8. O'Berry to Cameron, 16 May 1872, Cameron Family Papers, SHC.

9. Hale County, Deed Record Book X, pp. 614–15. The indenture between Cameron and Paul and James Hargress was originally made on 27 March 1876. They paid $8 per acre for 80 acres of land. Paul Hargress made a second purchase of 20 acres in 1884, for which he paid $10 per acre. Hale County, Deed Record Book K, p. 480.

10. Interview with Louis Rainey, August 1978 and July 1979.

11. Hale County, Deed Book X, pp. 616–17 (1912); Deed Book Y, pp. 2, 27, 83, 151, 213, 275, 449 (1912–13).

12. Interview with Louis Rainey, August 1979.

13. Interviews with Louis Rainey, August 1978, July 1979; interview with Betty Hargress Washington, August 1978.

14. His children give the date for Forrest Hargress's birth as 1 January 1866. The family Bible lists him as having been born on 1 January 1865, but the year is crossed out and "1866" is written over it. The *Greensboro Watchman*, which refused to carry news accounts of the 1965 voter-registration demonstrations in Selma, ran a front-page obituary column about Forrest Hargress upon his death in June 1965.

15. Interviews in August 1978 and July–August 1979, with Louis Rainey, Betty Hargress Washington, Angeline Hargress Banks, and Alice Hargress.

16. Interview with Louis Rainey, August 1978.

17. Interviews with Minnie Hargress Williams and Angeline Hargress Banks, August 1978; interview with Robert Cabbil, July 1979.

18. Interviews with Betty Hargress Washington, August 1978; interview with Louis Rainey, July 1979.

19. Interviews with Elijah Banks, August 1978 and August 1979; interviews with Robert Cabbil, July and August 1979; interview with Carrie Hargress Davis, August 1979.

20. Interviews with Louis Rainey, July and August 1979.

21. For a discussion of the world of the "rough and respectable" among working people of Victorian England, see Thompson 1973 and 1975. For the spiritual and the sinful on the plantation, see Epstein 1977. Kennedy 1973 presents an illuminating discussion of a quite different pattern of sexual mores, religious norms, and population practices among a society of small landowners and peasant proprietors.

22. Interviews with Louis Rainey, Joel Wallace, James and Lillie Mae Cannon, August 1979.

23. Interviews with Carrie Hargress Davis and with Joel Wallace, August 1979.

24. Interview with Alice Hargress, August 1978.

25. Interview with Elijah Banks, August 1979.

26. Interviews with Angeline Hargress Banks, Elijah Banks, Louis Rainey, and Alice Hargress, August 1979.

27. Interview with James Lyles, August 1979.

28. Interview with James Lyles, August 1979.

REFERENCES

Epstein, Dena J., 1977. *Sinful Tunes and Spirituals: Black Folk Music to the Civil War* (New York: Oxford University Press).

Gutman, Herbert, 1976. *The Black Family in Slavery and Freedom* (New York: Pantheon Books).

Kennedy, Robert E., Jr., 1973. *The Irish: Emigration, Marriage, and Fertility* (Berkeley: University of California Press).

Rosengarten, Theodore, 1974. *All God's Dangers: The Life of Nate Shaw* (New York: Alfred A. Knopf).

Thompson, Paul R., 1973. Voices from Within. In *The Victorian City: Images and Realities*, H. J. Dyos and Michael Wolff, eds. (London: Routledge and Kegan Paul), 1:59–80.

————, 1975. *The Edwardians: The Re-Making of British Society* (Bloomington: Indiana University Press).

Part Two

The Dynamics of Ritual and Conversion

The Conversion Ritual in a Rural Black Baptist Church

CHARLES WILLIAMS

Most rural southern black Baptist churches have the ritual process variously known as "getting religion" or "joining the church" that involves black youth and "sinners," the marginal members of the black Christian community. The symbolism of death and resurrection in this conversion process stems from the Biblical story of Jesus Christ experiencing a natural birth into a world of sin, being crucified, dying, and being resurrected—that is, being born again and ascending to heaven. Even though the main participants are young people, older Christians apparently look forward to revivals as much as, if not more than, the young. The conversion ritual—central to the revival activities held annually in many rural black churches—stands out vividly in my own mind for two reasons. First, I had to undergo this particular ritual in order to become a member of the North Side Baptist Church in Columbus, Mississippi, at the age of twelve. Secondly, I find many striking similarities between the conversion rituals I have observed and experienced and ethnographic descriptions of initiation rites in many African tribal societies. Although the argument for the persistence of African cultural elements in the United States is not fully developed in this essay, I believe that remnants of African initiation rituals may have been brought to this country by slaves, and later incorporated into the conversion ritual in many black churches in the antebellum South. Since the data reported in this paper derive from my own religious conversion experience, this effort also constitutes an experiment in the use of autobiographical material for ethnographic purposes.

According to Victor Turner, there are three stages in the initiation ritual, or "rite of passage": (1) separation, (2) margin, or limen, and (3) reaggregation (Turner 1974:196). Turner suggests that rituals are usually performed in societies (at all levels of social complexity) when individuals or groups are culturally defined as undergoing a change of status. These ceremonies often involve the isolation of adolescents from their families and younger children, circumcision, and initiation into full adult status within the group. The initiation ceremonies described by Turner display a number of similarities with the conversion ritual in rural black Baptist churches. In both settings the ceremonies center primarily on youth; the conversion ritual marks the social transition from the status of a child with few responsibilities to that of an adult with considerable responsibilities.

The conversion ritual is one of the strongest socializing forces operating upon youth in rural black communities for two reasons. First, it is only through conversion that they can become full members of their churches and of the black Christian community. Secondly, in such communities it is the only way young blacks can exercise voting powers in church matters, hold offices in various church organizations, and sing in the church choir. Generally, youth who have undergone the conversion ritual enjoy more prestige and status in the community than those who have not.

The usual scene for the conversion ritual is a camp meeting or revival. The ritual enacted at these sites serves both to socialize the young into Christianity and to renew the spirit of Christianity and commitment of older church members. Revivals do much to elevate the moral tone of the black community because they cleanse the community of "vices and unwanted foreign elements" that are considered bad for a Christian community. For decades, revivals have made the black community a spirit-filled entity conducive to the perpetuation of what I prefer to call "black religion."

Revivals in Lowndes County, Mississippi, usually occur in July and August, or at a time after church members have harvested their crops. In communities where there are several black churches, no two churches will schedule their revivals at the same time. One church takes the first week of the month, another the second week, and so forth. Such scheduling allows people from other churches and other communities to follow ceremonies from church to church. Many rural blacks find revivals to be intrinsically exciting events, and are motivated to attend, either because they fear not being saved or because they desire some stimulation and/or diversion. The revivals are held whether there are prospective conversion recruits or not. It is important to record and analyze these conversion rituals because they are dying out or losing their influence in many contemporary black communities.

During Sunday services several weeks before the revival, the preacher sets the stage by constantly reminding non-Christians (sinners): "You had better join the army of the Lord before it is too late." These admonishments are designed to strike fear in the hearts of nearly everyone: both sinners, whether backsliders or those who have never been converted, and hard-core members, who feel that they must get busy bringing new souls into the church to be saved. Parents, grandparents, and other relatives, therefore, seek out the remaining sinners in their families and in their neighborhoods to remind them that they will have to go to the "mourning bench," a literal bench or chairs—also known as the "anxious seat" and "sinner's seat"—where sinners during the revival pray for the salvation of their souls.

The conversion ritual was probably the most frightening experience of my childhood because I did not know exactly what to think or expect even after having watched my older brothers and sisters go through the same process. My parents and grandmother explained the rationale of the ceremony to me. I was one of a long line of sinners who were giving up their unclean souls for purification. I was born a sinner because of the sinful deeds of Adam and Eve, and now that I had reached the age of twelve, I would have to confess Jesus as my lord and savior and be saved in order to avoid God's wrath and a journey to hell. This explanation made things seem quite simple. All I had to do was stand before the preacher and congregation and repent of my sins and accept Jesus Christ as my savior. Lest I take this requirement too lightly, my grandmother—having noticed my visible sigh of relief—quickly emphasized that it was no easy task and that nothing could be taken for granted. I would have to give up playing baseball, watching television, riding a bicycle, playing with friends and relatives, reading comic books, and talking to friends on the telephone in order to remain secluded for several days before the conversion. Seclusion was the most fearful prospect of all because I had never been alone in my entire life. In African rituals, seclusion, one of the most important aspects of the conversion ritual, symbolizes death (Mbiti 1969:158). The rigors of "getting religion" seemed like a social death to me, frightening because it seemed to mean that I would have to be sad rather than happy, and punishing rather than rewarding.

In the remainder of this essay, I describe and analyze what I consider to be the six major steps in the conversion ritual. All of them must be completed before the prospective convert can become a member of the North Side Baptist Church. The six steps are as follows: (1) willingness to be saved, (2) seclusion, (3) occupying the mourning bench, (4) acceptance of Christ (testimony), (5) baptism, and (6) receiving the right hand of fellowship.

Step One: Willingness to Be Saved. The "sinner" must express a willingness to give up his or her childhood status and activities as a sinner and accept the new status and role of a Christian. The youth is about to change from passive membership to active membership in his community. Considerable social pressure is placed on the southern rural black child by his family, friends, and other church members if he does not take this initial step toward conversion. Although many young blacks readily accept this opportunity for public recognition, some families literally force their children into this ritual. In one instance, a child who had been forced to the mourners' bench by his parents informed the pastor during the ceremony that he was not ready to accept Christ because he did not want to stop having fun. Needless to say, the youth soon became an outcast in the community. The church deplores individuals, young and old, who refuse to accept the ways of Christ and instead seek fulfillment in worldly activities. Throughout my own conversion ritual experience, all "mourners" (prospective converts) were reminded of this particular case by the pastor, who referred to it each day during the revival services. Parents also told their children to expect ostracism if they followed their friend's example. Everyone in the church community predicted the worst for him and felt that he was damned to live the life of a sinner. The psychological pressures on me and the other prospective converts were so great that under no circumstances would we have dared to repeat his mistake.

All mourners must report to the church on the first night of the revival to take their place on the mourners' bench, where they are to search for a new Christian life. They also must report to the revival ceremony twice daily, at 11:00 A.M. and 7:00 P.M., throughout the remainder of the week of revival. The mourners may number from one to one hundred, and include both sexes and all ages. They are physically separated from the rest of the congregation. The necessary physical separation may be accomplished by having the mourners sit up front in regular church pews or in chairs arranged in a semicircle facing the pulpit (see Fig. 1).

Step Two: Seclusion. Mourners often are secluded from activities and people that may interfere with their concentration on preparing to accept Christ and his teachings. This phase is analogous to the stage in African rituals during which "novices are secluded from the scenes of their preliminal activities and social interactions in such wild or hidden sites as forest or caves" (Turner 1974:196). This stage symbolizes the death of the old body and of sin. The strict regimen of nonparticipation in such activities as riding bicycles and watching television has already been described. Whenever the mourners are not at the church taking part in the revival, they are to seclude themselves in order to pray and sing because seclusion is supposed to be an ideal way to communicate with God. Many mourners who live in rural areas enter the forest for isolation and prayer—to receive visions from God. Those who live in more populous areas usually retreat to closets, vacant rooms, woodsheds, and attics. In order to assist the mourner, parents may restrict his or her chores and errands to the home. I sat with my grandmother and discussed the meaning of the Christian religion, God, and the Bible. These discussions were always conducted in a serious vein, and such seemingly frivolous questions as "How do you know there is a God?" or "Have you seen God?" were not allowed. When I was undergoing conversion, for example, I helped my father repair our damaged front porch and mowed lawns for our neighbors. I was never permitted outside of the neighborhood during the conversion period. When my sister went through the same ritual several years before me, she did not go outside of the house except to attend the revival services. This is probably the most trying time of all for mourners because, despite the communal context of the conversion ritual, the actual encounter with the divine being is unique and intensely personal for each individual. In fact, I have never met any Baptist

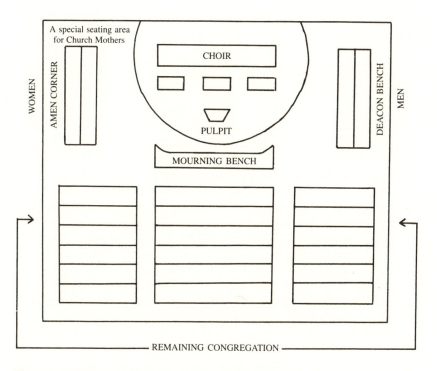

Figure 1. A diagram of a typical rural black Baptist Church.

who did not claim absolute uniqueness for his or her encounter with the Holy Spirit. For some mourners the experience of "getting religion" resembles trauma: they sometimes cry hysterically, shout, scream, fall down and roll on the floor, laugh, jerk, and bark like animals. During seclusion, visions and other unexplainable occurrences may affect mourners. People might say, "I know God is real because He came to me one Thursday evening when I was praying in the woods." Such statements represent capsule testaments made by individuals who had "gotten happy" during their youth. When "getting religion," some individuals who normally are shy and self-conscious shed those characteristics and act "abnormally" according to standards set by the larger society. Naive investigators too often have dismissed the ecstatic-possession states exhibited by black Americans as "crude Negro emotionalism." Such views are usually expressed by observers with little understanding of either religious phenomena or Afro-Americans.

Among the most valuable aspects of these ritual ceremonies is the socializing effect they have upon black youth. The surprisingly strong impact of the conversion ritual is reflected in the attitudinal and behavioral changes of many so-called misguided youth. Religion in many small black communities is, therefore, a strong means of social control.

Step Three: Occupying the Mourning Bench. While they sit on the mourning bench, mourners receive prayers from the congregation and spiritual guidance from sermons of the resident preacher and visiting preachers. The mourners also must pray for the salvation of their own souls.

The main activities during the revival service are praying, singing, and preaching. Contrary to descriptions of some earlier writers, there is never a monetary collection until the close of the revival services. Each service is opened with a reading of scripture that reflects the activity at hand. When children are on the mourner's bench, for example, the scripture might be Matthew 19:14 ("Suffer little children . . . to come unto me"). In fact, every reading, testimony, prayer, sermon, and song is chosen especially for the conversion ritual. After the scripture is read by one deacon, another may lead the prayer, the theme of which sets the tone for the conversion ritual. The prayer usually involves thanking God for everybody's presence; for food, clothing, and shelter; and, most of all, for having sent the mourners to his house. The prayer is followed by such "soul-stirring" songs as "I Know I've Got Good Religion in My Heart" or "Give Me That Old-Time Religion." These rhythmical and meaningful revival songs provoke participants to clap their hands, tap their feet, or even shout for joy.

During the scripture and first prayer, only the mourners are required to kneel, and they must kneel for every prayer thereafter. The scripture, first prayer, and first song are known as the devotional segment of the service. The devotion is used in all black rural southern religious services and even in some secular group meetings.

There may be several prayers and songs following the initial devotion before the preacher takes over the service. The prayers may be led by people from the congregation, including, but not restricted to, parents, relatives, and friends of persons on the mourning bench. When I was a participant in this ritual, both my father and grandmother came to the bench and prayed with me while the congregation sang. When the prayers are completed, the preacher states that he feels the presence of the spirit of God, and he begins a fire-and-brimstone sermon. The preacher sometimes leaves the pulpit while delivering these spirit-filled sermons and preaches from the mourning bench. The congregation responds by saying "Amen," clapping their hands, and shouting and praising God.

Following the sermon, the preacher asks the mourners whether God has manifested Himself to them and whether they are willing to accept God and Jesus Christ as their savior. When I was a mourner, I was questioned in this way by the minister, but I did not respond because I was too nervous and did not know what to say. The answer he was seeking was more than a simple "yes"; he wanted a complete testimony and verification of God's appeal to me. The other mourners and I did not respond during the first two nights of revival, but later in the week at least half of the mourners gave testimonies. I was unfortunate to be in the last half of the group to be converted because, while the first mourners to be converted received praise and congratulations, the remaining ones received only more pressure from their parents, relatives, and friends to accept Christ. To make matters worse, the mourners who had already been converted were separated from the nonconverts, thereby creating joy for the new converts and sadness for those of us who had not yet been converted. The preacher closed the revival service one night near the end of revival week by encouraging us unconverted mourners to remove all play from our hearts and to pray even more vigorously for the remaining days of the revival so that we, too, might be converted.

The same general cycle of activities was repeated throughout the entire week until all of the mourners were converted. Only then was the revival considered a complete success and a blessing from God. The congregation would have felt blessed to have had even one person converted, but to have all twelve "sinners" converted was a special blessing and confirmation that God was pleased with the good works of the preacher and of the church during the revival services.

Step Four: Acceptance of Christ (testimony). This aspect of the conversion ritual is much more complex than earlier researchers recognized. It is not easy to determine whether one has received Christ because it is thought to be a personal and private relationship between the mourner and Christ; no one else can know when this relationship is finally felt. A mourner may accept Christ—or "get religion"—during one of the seclusion stages when he is totally alone. Or he may actually accept Christ during the mourning bench ceremony at the church. Nonbelievers who question the authenticity of "getting religion" take an untenable position as far as church members are concerned. The members feel that they alone have experienced the religious and ritual phenomena that they describe; consequently, they alone can appreciate what is involved in that experience.

Whenever "getting religion" takes place—whether in seclusion or on the mourning bench—mourners must notify the congregation at the next revival service by giving testimony of the experience. Usually the preacher asks the mourner whether he now has religion. If the response is "yes," the mourner must tell how God has converted his life of sin to a life of Christian joy, and pledge himself to be a devoted, faithful Christian. At this point many mourners are so filled with emotion that they often shed tears and shout, "I am so glad, I am so glad I've got good religion." The preacher then will console the mourner and ask him to tell the congregation when the "Spirit of God" came to him. After each mourner, through his testimony, has convinced the preacher and congregation of his conversion, the preacher asks the deacons to come forward to vote together with the congregation on the legitimacy of each individual conversion. The entire church usually votes "yes" in each case. Then all converted mourners are told to stand beside the preacher so that he might show newcomers and the congregation the number that have "gotten religion" during the revival, as well as inform the mourners and congregation of the date of the baptismal ceremony. (For published accounts of the acceptance of Christ stage, see Woodson 1921:16.)

My grandmother once told me that when she was converted and the Spirit entered her body, everything around her looked new, including her own physical appearance. In other words, she was saying that the Spirit had given her a new body, a Christian body, by driving out sin, her former body. To keep her Christian body new she had to continue to serve God according to his will. Symbolically, the old body represents death, whereas the new body represents the rebirth of life. Belief in the newness of a recent convert's surroundings is similar to a concept held by some African societies. According to Mbiti (1969:158–59), "the process of dying, living in the spirit world and being reborn (resurrected) . . . is the act of rejoining their families, which emphasizes and dramatizes that the young people are now new, they have new personalities, they have lost their childhood."

Frazier (1940:113) published the following account of "getting religion" experienced by a black American female: "It was in 1931. I had always been taught to pray. In this Baptist revival I sang and prayed. I prayed and people prayed for me. Finally I felt happy. I saw some people shouting: I wanted to shout too, but I couldn't bring myself to it. All I could do was cry. I almost doubted religion when I first got it."

The intense subjectivity of this and other accounts supports the notion that each conversion experience is, in some respects, unique. "Getting religion" is an individual pursuit, and just as personalities differ so do the religious experiences persons encounter. There are no prescribed rules—except for the stages of the conversion ritual outlined herein.

Step Five: Baptism. Symbolically baptism represents purification from the states of sin, uncleanliness, wrongness, and evil. During this process the preacher submerges the converts one at a time in water—usually the shallows of a river, lake, or pool. Here similarities between southern black Baptist conversion and African initiation rites diminish, for rather than using water to baptize, many African societies use special knives for circumcision or clitoridectomy. On the Sunday when baptizing is scheduled, new converts are exceedingly happy because the worst part of the conversion ritual is behind them, and they soon will return to a life of normal social interaction. The converts are also happy for other reasons: they know what the baptizing ceremony entails because they have seen others being baptized, and their parents, relatives, and peers are also happy. Everyone seems to smile on this glorious day and wears his or her best clothes for the occasion. Many converts are further pleased because their parents have purchased new clothes to adorn their new spiritual bodies.

In the early morning hours prior to the baptizing, the deacons prepare an area for the ceremony and church services to follow. At the church converts are dressed in long white gowns tied at the feet. Their heads are covered with white handkerchiefs. The preacher usually dons a white or black robe; his head may or may not be covered. Once the congregation has arrived at the water, the preacher is led into the water by two deacons who will continue to assist the preacher throughout the ceremony. (Because of the danger to converts who do not know how to swim, many rural black churches now are building shallow, concrete pools inside the church or on grounds near the church.)

Either the preacher or one of the deacons reads a scripture before the baptizing ceremony. After the reading, the other deacon leads the congregation in prayer and song while the first deacon takes the hand of the convert and stands beside him or her. Then the preacher places one hand on the convert's back; the other hand, wrapped in a towel, covers the convert's face. Just before the submerging, the preacher says, "Brother ———— or Sister ————, I now will baptize you in the name of the Father, the Son, and the Holy Ghost." The convert then is submerged in three or four feet of water, and may come up shouting, "Hallelujah, Hallelujah" or "Thank you, Jesus; thank you, Jesus." After all of the converts have been baptized in this manner, they hurriedly change into dry clothes. The preacher and deacons also change clothes. Parents and friends in the congregation bring out food and drink because it is customary to have dinner on the church grounds following baptism. During the baptizing everyone is very solemn and serious, but immediately after the ceremony is completed they may laugh, smile, and even joke. The choir sings a combination of church hymns and black spirituals. The new converts are encouraged to join in the singing since they now are fellow Christians and full members of the church.

Throughout the evening following the baptizing, new converts feel relieved, cleansed, and chosen. For a long time thereafter each new convert will be acutely aware of his words and actions. Although a few converts stray from the "path of righteousness," most remain faithful throughout their lives. Converts seldom deviate from prescribed Christian doctrine because the adult black community considers "getting religion" and maintaining appropriate behavior to be terribly serious matters; consequently, they socialize their children to believe as they believe.

Baptism by immersion is limited to adults and to children old enough to understand the meaning of the conversion ritual, usually twelve years of age.

Baptists look upon immersion as "realistic symbolism," embodying the burial of a life of sin for a new life grounded in a faith in God (Rosten 1952:346). This ritual was first performed by John the Baptist, who appeared in the Judean wilderness preaching a baptism of repentance for the forgiveness of sins and telling his followers, "I indeed have baptized you with water: but he [God] shall baptize you with the Holy Ghost" (Mark 1:4–8). According to the scriptures, Jesus Christ was also baptized by John the Baptist in the River Jordan. On the basis of this ritual undergone by Jesus Christ, American Baptists believe that immersion in water follows the teachings of the Bible.

Step Six: Receiving the Right Hand of Fellowship. The final stage of the conversion ritual is receiving the "right hand of fellowship." This ceremony is held in the evening following the baptismal ceremony. During my own conversion experience, some older Christians jokingly told the new converts, "Don't lose your religion before you receive the right hand of fellowship."

Although the origins of the right hand of fellowship are not clearly documented in the doctrine of the Baptist Church, most black Baptist churches have formalized it as a very significant stage of the conversion ritual. I have discussed the nature of this particular ritual with several black ministers and lay Christians. Although they, too, were vague about its origins, they all agreed that it was basically a welcoming into the church of new converts and also "one Christian disciple extending a hand of goodwill or fellowship to another Christian brother or sister."

This part of the conversion ritual takes place in the evening following the baptismal exercise. Plumpp (1972:15–17) described the process as follows: "Following the sermon and the collection, the pastor asks all new converts to stand and come forward. When all the converts are standing in a straight line in front of the congregation, the pastor will ask the congregation to come and give the new Christians 'the Right Hand of Fellowship.'" Although the ceremony appears to some observers to be no more than the whole congregation marching forward behind the pastor to shake hands with the new converts, it means everlasting brotherhood between two Christians; it signifies that young sinners finally have been accepted into the army of God as Christians; and most importantly, it means that the new converts have the same rights and privileges as any other member of the church regardless of age or standing. He or she can now vote in the affairs of the church and can hold any office in the church organizations. During the fellowship ceremony, which usually lasts about half an hour, one convert may shake the hands of as many as 500 people. Despite the probable soreness of the hand, the converts usually are very happy because it is their day to be honored.

This ceremony was very meaningful in my own life. And I hope that this heavily autobiographical account of the entire experience will stand as my own peculiar sort of personal, as well as anthropological, testimony.

REFERENCES

Frazier, E. Franklin, 1940. *Negro Youth at the Crossways* (Washington, D.C.: American Council on Education).

May, Herbert G., and Bruce M. Metzger, 1973. *The New Oxford Annotated Bible with the Apocrypha* (New York: Oxford University Press).

Mbiti, John S., 1969. *African Religions and Philosophy* (New York: Praeger).

Plumpp, Sterling D., 1972. *Black Rituals* (Chicago: Third World Press).

Rosten, Leo, 1952. *Religions in America* (New York: Harcourt, Brace).

Turner, Victor, 1974. *Dramas, Fields and Metaphors* (Ithaca: Cornell University Press).

Woodson, Carter G., 1921. *History of the Negro Church* (Washington, D.C.: Associated Publishers).

The Role of Aesthetics in the Conversion Experience in a Missionary Baptist Church

JOHN A. FORREST

Members of a Missionary Baptist church in the swamplands of northeastern North Carolina have made many changes in the physical appearance of their church since it was first built in the 1890s and sheathed in white clapboard. These and other changes in the aesthetic realm of the church may influence the behavior of members of this church community. In this paper I explore the possibility that the aesthetic realm is not simply a manifestation of other social facts, but is actually interdependent with them and may in turn be efficacious in guiding behavior. Anthropologists and philosophers alike have argued that there is a sharp distinction between the aesthetic and functional aspects of objects (Maquet 1971; Stolnitz 1960; Vivas 1937). Using field data from an intensive study of an ethnically white Missionary Baptist church in a northeast North Carolina fishing community, I intend to show that "aesthetic" and "functional" are not mutually exclusive categories.

This paper is divided into two parts. First I will present data taken from my own field research and attempt to show how the aesthetic realm can be, or is thought to be, an aid in guiding behavior. The ultimate aim of this research is to define an aesthetic community as more than a group of people whose aesthetic judgments are similar, or even a group of people who share the same criteria for making aesthetic judgments. I wish to show that the people in an aesthetic community are united by the effects of the aesthetic realm on their behavior and by their manipulation of the aesthetic realm to alter behavior. In the second part of the paper I shall consider some broader issues in the theory of aesthetics. These issues include ways of ordering the data and the general problem of distinguishing between the aesthetic and the nonaesthetic aspects of things. It is my hope that the reader will be able to utilize the concrete data presented in the first part of the paper as a backdrop for the more abstract and theoretical discussion of the aesthetic realm that follows.

I

As one part of a larger, year-long field study conducted in the swamplands of northeast North Carolina during 1978, I focused intensively on a single church community. Locally this church is considered the most important single institution for the maintenance of social cohesion. It is the only institution in the larger community that draws its members from a wide variety of social backgrounds and includes all ages. Furthermore, the church members believe that social solidarity can be achieved only through adherence to fundamental Christian moral principles. Therefore they feel that the more members the church can attract, the greater will be the social solidarity in the larger community from which it draws. The business of attracting new members is pertinent to the issues under discussion.

The look of the church building itself is both an index of local religious preferences and an aid to organizing behavior within the building. Anyone reasonably familiar with southern church architecture and decor would be able to tell from the interior of this building that it is a southern Missionary Baptist church. Cues include central choir loft and pulpit placement, dark sanctuary, spare but not spartan furnishings, limited use of plain-colored glass in narrow peaked windows, and twin-aisle pew placement. The appointments of the sanctuary mark it off not only as a place of worship, but also as a place in which only certain kinds of worship behavior are acceptable.

Visual, nonperformance, nondescriptive aesthetic forms "set the stage," as it were, for desired behavior. To create the desired environment it is convenient to use aesthetic forms that are constantly present and that can be perceived in their totality at any time—that is, nonperformance forms. Preferably the forms should be perceived by a sense that is highly significant cognitively and affectively—either sight or hearing. Since hearing cannot be effectively used in a nonperformance way, sight is the only choice. All forms need not be nondescriptive, although for doctrinal reasons they are in this case.

Sacred space can be bounded using nonvisual forms, but they have disadvantages. The heat of a campfire or the sound of a musical instrument can define a space, but the spaces bounded by these forms are not discrete because nonvisual forms do not act as perimeters but emanate from a central source; they pervade the space that they define. By moving farther and farther from the source, a person perceives the nonvisual form less and less until eventually it can no longer be perceived. A person "outside" of the space bounded by a nonvisual form is simply denied certain sensations. Visual forms can encircle a space such that those people in the space perceive one thing and those outside of it perceive something totally different. The exterior look of a building is not simply the absence of the interior look; it is qualitatively different. Buildings can be designed so that the exterior gives the observer clues enabling him to predict what he will find inside, or so that the exterior belies the interior. The latter, for culturally significant reasons, is the case for the church building under discussion.

When the church was built by the founding members in 1895, it was a simple edifice. It was constructed out of the same kind of materials used for most dwellings at that time. The building was essentially rectangular with a gabled roof and two symmetrically placed doors in the gabled end that faces the road. The whole was sheathed in white clapboard. The interior walls and ceiling were dressed with a lath-like paneling and finished with a special palm oil. The members have always liked the look of the interior and have vehemently opposed any attempts to change it. But in the 1950s it was generally agreed that the exterior had to be changed. Both the interior and the exterior looked old, but it was felt that the interior signs of age were aesthetically pleasing whereas the exterior ones were not: the exterior was "shabby" and "old-fashioned," while the interior was "antique." The members decided to brick-veneer the exterior in order to make the church look more "established" and prosperous. To complete this image, a bell tower and steeple were added, and the twin front doors were replaced by a single central entrance.

Until the 1950s very few outsiders came to or passed through the town. The region in which it is located is mostly deep swamp and low-lying; by and large, it is poorly drained farmland. Although a reasonably efficient road system was constructed in the 1930s, there was little reason for outsiders to visit the area. But after 1950 the tourist trade steadily increased, some coming to town for hunting and fishing, others passing through on the way to the Outer Banks of North Carolina. Also at that time the church hired its first full-time preacher, where previously it had been part of a four-church circuit. I suggest that the aesthetic changes made to the exterior of the church were prompted by these social changes and served three related functions. Although the members liked their humble little country church, they were not anxious for outsiders to view it as such. Until the massive influx of tourists this was not an issue. The members also wished to attract outsiders and new residents to attend the church, but felt that the old exterior gave the impression of a poor and poorly attended church that was not particularly inviting. Finally, the church is not especially well-endowed and cannot afford a large stipend for a preacher. When reviewing potential candidates for preacher, however, the members do not wish to have this aspect of the church immediately obvious from the building's exterior. Thus, the exterior of the church building obscures certain aspects of the church that the members do not wish to be public.

Regular services at the church serve two main functions: to provoke non-members to come forward and be baptized and to reinforce the beliefs of the members present. I shall concentrate on the former function here. The beginning and end of each service are signaled by choral music, thereby marking the intervening period as a time for special behavior and special attention. In particular, the members of the congregation should act in unison—sitting, standing, singing, and talking as one.

Although choral music—an aural, descriptive, performance form—is used as a temporal marker to define a special time, other forms using other senses could be employed. To mark the beginning of a service, for example, a light could be turned on, a censer could be brought in, or the heat could be turned up. But cues of this sort would merely indicate that the service had begun. The choral music is descriptive. It contains a message about what is expected of the congregation. The words of the call to worship, taken from Habakkuk 2:20, suggest that the following time should be marked by subdued behavior: "The Lord *is* in his holy temple: let all the earth keep silence before him." Although these same words could be expressed in a nonchoral way, the choral music signifies order and unity better than mere speaking or writing. Not only is the choral music an overt act of unity, with every member of the choir singing the same words at the same time, but it is also an act that creates order out of diversity. Each voice section of the choir sings a different tonal line that blends with the others to form a harmonic whole.

The major aesthetic forms of the service are music and oratory. Since the members hire and fire the preacher and music director through the democratic process, they have considerable control over these forms and have strict principles about what is acceptable. The choral music of the church is marked by controlled singing with clear enunciation. The choral pieces are not elaborately harmonized works, but hymnlike in form and harmony. The music is considered by members to be aesthetically in accord with the physical surroundings, and also expressive of, and *conducive to*, appropriate behavior. Both the music and the surroundings are subdued; they are not, however, starkly plain, overly controlled, or without individual flourishes.

Some years ago a music director, in conjunction with the preacher, introduced a different style of music that was of the camp-meeting or pentecostal style, marked by free, uncontrolled singing in an antiphonal manner. This innovation created a major controversy in the congregation which ultimately resulted in the resignation of the music director and the preacher. The new music was believed to promote spontaneous outbursts of emotion from people—behavior that is considered undesirable. Therefore this music could not be tolerated.

According to church members, the sermon also should be stylistically in keeping with the other aesthetic forms mentioned. Sermons should be neither overly emotional nor delivered in a manner suggesting uncontrolled absorption with its content, yet they should be vocally well modulated. One of the main functions of the sermon is to cause nonmembers to come forward. But it is believed that this act cannot be brought about by a simple appeal to reason, since many of the statements that the preacher asks nonmembers to believe are not considered to be subject to rational analysis. Many of these statements involve apparent logical contradictions: death is not death; Jesus of Nazareth was fully God and fully human; God is one and God is three. By all tenets of Western logic it is irrational to hold contradictory beliefs. If appeal to reason were all that was needed to bring about conversion, the service would be unnecessary. One simple, carefully worded logical argument would suffice. But this is not the case; conversion involves a change in affective state and must be brought about through affect.

Various affecting genres are employed to increase the chances of persuading a nonmember to come forward. The visual, nonperformance, nondescriptive aspects of the surroundings are stylistically similar to, and work in conjunction with, the aural, performance, and descriptive aspects of the actual service. Taste, smell, and touch cannot reasonably be employed, since their relationships to cognitive processes and physical actions are suspect in this context. One could, for example, offer a steak dinner at the pulpit or use a cattle prod to induce someone to come forward. Although no one can ever be sure that the person who comes forward at a normal service has "genuinely" undergone a conversion experience, it could be reasonably assumed that most of those who came forward for a culinary reward or to end a painful physical sensation had not. Church members generally think of humans as being divided into body, mind, and soul. Taste, smell, and touch primarily influence the body, whereas sight and hearing influence not only the body but also the mind and soul; and in the service it is believed that they influence mind and soul almost exclusively.

The part of the service that actually provokes nonmembers to come forward—the invitational part of the sermon and the hymn of invitation—are aural, performance, descriptive forms. By using performance forms, attention is focused. It is also important to use descriptive forms, such as the invitation and the hymn of invitation, that are specifically *about* coming forward and leave no doubt as to what action is expected. Thus we have two sets of aesthetic forms, stylistically unified and working in conjunction, to help evoke desired behavior. The visual, nonperformance, nondescriptive forms create an environment in which the aural, descriptive, performance forms command attention. Distraction is minimized by keeping as many cognitive, affective, and sensual areas as possible busy with the matter at hand.

Services held without these aesthetic forms are fragmentary and difficult to control. Baptisms performed in a stretch of water near the church are cases in point. People come and go as they please; some sit while others stand; some are attentive, while others talk among themselves. The preacher was greatly dissatisfied with this method of baptism primarily for that reason. The attitude of the congregation was casual and jocular when he felt that this crucial rite of passage should have been more solemn and given undivided attention. The preacher's verbal commands for attention were insufficient. Without the aesthetic realm on his side, his ability to guide the behavior of others was significantly reduced.

I maintain that this church community is also an aesthetic community. The members' aesthetic judgments are largely in agreement, and they agree about the criteria for making aesthetic judgments. The behavior of the members is also influenced by the aesthetic realm, and members agree on how the aesthetic realm can or should be used to influence behavior.

II

The first theoretical issue addressed in this essay is the identification of the aesthetic realm itself. Morris Weitz (1956), following a line of reasoning proposed by Wittgenstein (1953:31–36), suggests that "art" is an *open concept*: it cannot be defined in terms of necessary and sufficient conditions. No matter how we try to define "art," artists can always create objects that are undeniably works of art but do not meet the defining criteria. Weitz suggests that instead of trying to define "art" one should attempt to characterize it by first enumerating examples of objects that people generally agree are art, and then extrapolating from them to those about which there is some doubt. In a similar fashion the aesthetic realm can be characterized as the totality of the aesthetic aspects of human and natural creations. Examples include gingerbread on a house, the birdcalls in Beethoven's *Pastoral Symphony*, and the taste of coq au vin. Instead of listing tens of thousands of aesthetic aspects of things and using this list as a basis for making decisions on new cases, it is simpler to give some empirical—although not universal—generalizations about these aesthetic aspects. The aesthetic aspects of things are capable of being perceived sensually, capable of being appreciated without reference to their utility, open to value judgements, and subject to opinions based on personal taste.

These empirical generalizations are not necessary and sufficient conditions for the aspect to be dubbed "aesthetic." Conceptual art, for example, has obvious aesthetic aspects, but it cannot be perceived sensually. I am not suggesting that all aspects of objects that display all of these features are necessarily aesthetic aspects.

One of the characteristics of the aesthetic realm—namely, its capacity to be appreciated disinterestedly—is important but subject to misunderstanding. A "capacity to be appreciated disinterestedly" means that an aspect of a thing may be attended to and/or appreciated without reference to the thing's usefulness as an agent in a temporal means/end or cause/effect sequence. Simply stated, the aesthetic aspect of something is capable of being appreciated for its own sake. This does not mean that the thing with an aesthetic aspect cannot be used as a means to an end, nor does it mean that the aspect is necessarily devoid of utility; far from it. Several examples may clarify the point. According to Schneider (1956:104), the Pakot of Kenya consider the lip on a milk jug "beautiful" or "pleasing to contemplate." This same lip facilitates pouring milk from the jug. The shape of the lip is both aesthetically pleasing and useful, but these two aspects of the same object, while structurally identical, must be treated differently. The look of the lip does not cause a Pakot to pour milk from the jug. Yet the aesthetic aspect of a thing may be used as a means to an end. The taste of a particular food may be pleasing in itself without regard to the nutritional value of the food. Because the pleasing taste may prompt a diner to eat heartily, parents often try to lure their children into eating nutritionally valuable foods by making them taste good. In this case the taste is both pleasing and useful.

It is convenient analytically to distinguish three features of the aesthetic aspect of things: (1) the sense used to perceive the aspect; (2) whether or not the aspect is an aspect of something that we might call "descriptive"; and (3) whether or not the aspect is an aspect of something that is performed.

Since one of the characteristics of the aesthetic aspects of things is their capability of being perceived sensually, it is reasonable to group them according to the principal sense employed. One can test for the principal sense by thinking of a thing with an aesthetic aspect and then imagining oneself deprived of each sense in turn. In almost all cases there is a crucial sense without which a thing can only be appreciated aesthetically to a minimal degree, if at all. In some cases the test is difficult or indecisive. However, since the analysis that attempts to categorize in this way need not deal with problem cases, further discussion is unnecessary.

Each sense has particular properties and particular limitations. These properties or limitations are important when an aesthetic aspect that relies heavily on one sense is used as a means to an end. Sperber's thoughts about the olfactory sense in *Rethinking Symbolism* (1975:115–18) are informative on this point. The olfactory nerves of the average human are capable of distinguishing hundreds of thousands of smells. Despite this remarkable ability, we in the West have virtually no way of referring to smells except by indicating their source (the smell of new-mown hay, the smell of a rose) or their effect (a mouth-watering smell, a nauseating smell). Also, it is nearly impossible to mentally conjure up the smell of something, whereas it is easy to picture something red or hexagonal. Even so, our ability to recognize smells can be acute. Smells from the past dredge up old memories, evoking a slew of associations. This strongly suggests that the relationship between the olfactory sense and human cognitive and affective processes differs from that of the other senses. This special relationship may limit the functional use of the sense.

Some things that have an aesthetic aspect could be called "descriptive" or "representational." A novel may describe an event, or a painting may be a representation of a person. There is a test using ordinary language that makes clearer the meaning of description or representation. The following sentences make this distinction nicely:

1. A is a B of a C.
2. A is a B about a C.
3. A is a B of a C and about a D.

These can be exemplified:

1. Rodin's *Le Penseur* is a statue of a man.
2. *Madam Butterfly* is an opera about a Japanese woman's love for an American sailor.
3. Giotto's *Kiss of Judas* is a fresco of a man kissing another man and is about a biblical event.

The key concepts here are "of-ness" and "about-ness." Statues, novels, and poems can be of or about something in a way that chairs, buildings, and spoons cannot. If someone were to design a chair in the shape of a hand it would be incorrect to say:

1. This is a chair of a hand.
2. This is a chair about a hand.

The relationship between the perceiver and the perceived differs depending on whether or not the thing with an aesthetic aspect is "of" or "about" something.

Finally, we can distinguish the performed from the nonperformed. Some forms of art are conventionally styled "lively" or "performing" arts. Since this notion is well known, there is no need to dwell on it. One point, however, should be made. Perception of a lively work involves a relatively fixed commitment of time and attention, whereas perception of a nonlively work does not. One can truthfully claim to have seen half of the film *Gone With the Wind* without evoking comment concerning meaning, but the claim to have seen half of Giotto's *Kiss of Judas* needs explaining.

Although demonstration of the full heuristic value of this analytic framework is too long a task to undertake here, it is my hope that the presentation of the field data gives initial credence to the approach. That is, I hope that the analysis of the field data shows that the aesthetic realm may be, or is thought to be, efficacious in guiding behavior. Grouping aesthetic aspects according to the taxonomy outlined above helps explain how different aesthetic aspects are useful in different circumstances for guiding behavior.

REFERENCES

Maquet, Jacques, 1971. *Introduction to Aesthetic Anthropology* (Cambridge, Mass.: Addison-Wesley).
Schneider, Harold K., 1956. The Interpretation of Pakot Visual Art. *Man* 56:103–6.
Sperber, Dan, 1975 (trans. Alice L. Morton). *Rethinking Symbolism* (Cambridge: Cambridge University Press).
Stolnitz, Jerome, 1960. *Aesthetics and Philosophy of Art Criticism* (Boston: Houghton Mifflin).
Vivas, Eliseo, 1937. A Definition of Esthetic Experience. *Journal of Philosophy* 34:628–34.
Weitz, Morris, 1956. The Role of Theory in Aesthetics. *Journal of Aesthetics and Art Criticism* 15:27–35.
Wittgenstein, Ludwig, 1953 (trans. G. E. M. Anscombe). *Philosophical Investigations* (Oxford: Oxford University Press).

The Religious Interpretation of Experience in a Rural Black Community

BRUCE T. GRINDAL

In this examination of the religious life of a rural black community in north Florida, I wish to stress the highly personal quality of religiosity, in which the authority of religious conviction lies in *feeling* and, at its most intimate level, exists independently of church affiliation or membership. Particular attention is given to the quality of personal experiences and to the interpretations accorded these experiences through examination of the life histories of people from various segments of the community. Attention is also focused on the individual's involvement in the church, since its activities and ritual events provide the context in which individual experience is translated into the symbolic meanings of communal religion.

First, I shall briefly examine the history and livelihood of the Midway community with special consideration given to the churches and attendant social life. Although in many respects Midway shares the rural poverty and racial inequality that has historically defined the black culture of the deep South, Midway people also exhibit strong historical pride and are modestly affluent by comparison with other areas of the rural South.

In this paper I shall also examine various factors contributing to the uniqueness of black religion: an African heritage and the institutions of slavery and racism. The concepts of God and Devil are representations of the universal human experience involving deeper conceptualizations of personal purity and the overall existence of order and justice in the world. As symbolic manifestations of opposed principles, God and Devil are intimately related to the experiential world of blacks, and particularly to racism and the numerous dichotomies it imposes.

The Midway community is located within a predominantly rural county in north Florida. Over 95 percent of its 2,000 residents are black. Although some inhabit a small, centralized village area, the majority live in loosely scattered hamlets covering an area of 25 square miles. The vegetation is characteristically longleaf pine and slash pine forests, and the soils of the area are sandy upland and red-clay hummock. Where this highly fertile soil has been cleared, it supports an important part of the people's livelihood—usually in the form of small gardens that augment the diets of separate households.

As its name suggests, the community is located midway between the county seat and a minor city in the neighboring county. Both are a distance of 15 miles, and they are connected to the community by a state highway and a railroad freight line. While subsistence farming and local industry do exist, most of the people are wage laborers in neighboring towns. This unincorporated area is provided with such services as police protection, rural electrification, and schools by the county. Community life—in the sense of collective participation—is defined almost solely by the interlocking activities of Midway's ten churches.

The earliest historical accounts of the Midway community date to the 1850s, when a relatively autonomous black slave population had already begun to establish small and informal church congregations pastored by visiting preachers from the county seat (Gearhart 1956:329). These preachers, usually white and educated, also taught the children basic reading skills. There is evidence from both white and black sources that by 1869 the area accommodated many ex-slave ministers who, without formal religious training, ministered to small congregations and at revivals (Richardson 1963:147). Following the war these congregations first established autonomy under ex-slave preachers and later formalized when the national conventions of black churches began to impact the area.

The beginnings of church affiliation were closely tied to the traditional tenure of land in the community. Following emancipation, many blacks homesteaded and acquired land; others were able to sharecrop, and by offering up a certain amount of their harvest, were able gradually to acquire land. By the end of the century, the community was made up of small independent farmers living on the subsistence of their gardens. Cotton and tobacco also were grown, and the railway station built in 1900 afforded the black population an opportunity to market these commodities and obtain cash payments for the goods. The population of the village, however, remained quite small throughout the nineteenth century, and the separate households tended to group in hamlets. The residents of these hamlets composed the early church congregations.

The building of a fuller's earth mine in 1915, along with the subsequent establishment of turpentine and lumber industries during the first quarter of this century, brought about considerable change in the community. Current residents—mostly males—went to work in the industries. In addition, a large number of migrants came to work, and many remained, settling in the community with their families. During the 1920s, over 1,000 individuals were employed in the local industries, and the life of the community shifted from rural hamlets to the central community. At this time, the area supported its largest population and experienced its greatest affluence; the first schools were built, and were staffed by black teachers. The geographic mobility created by these industries, as well as the improvement of roads, allowed greater contact with neighboring towns and bettered chances for wage employment. This did not seriously alter the settlement and tenure patterns of landowning blacks, however. Most continued to live on their farms, with the bulk of the work within the family shifting from the husband to the wife and children.

During the depression in the 1930s, when the mines, sawmills, and turpentine distilleries closed, most of the local residents returned to subsistence farming. Some migrated to major cities in Florida, such as Fort Lauderdale, while others moved to cities in the North. With the outbreak of World War II, many of the youth joined the armed forces, thus hastening the population exodus. Finally, the closing of the train depot and Western Union office after the war once again isolated the community commercially and geographically and increased its poverty.

During the 1950s the community continued to experience slow but steady out-migration. Since the late 1960s, however, a period of relative affluence and growth has emerged. Many of the practical racial barriers lessened as a result of federal legislation that outlawed blatantly racist injustices. Rural electrification and improved opportunities for wage employment in neighboring towns have led to a noticeable rise in living standards. Many young people who formerly would have migrated to the cities now are staying home, often purchasing trailers with their savings and moving them onto their parents' land.

Today the Midway community has ten churches. In terms of membership, the two largest denominations are the Colored Primitive Baptist and the African Methodist Episcopal; each has three churches located in separate areas of the community. The African Methodist Episcopal churches were founded shortly after the Civil War, the first in 1867 by a group of affiliated laymen, and the other two during the 1870s. Currently the African Methodist Episcopal churches have but one minister among them who serves the churches on different Sundays of the month. Although the governance of the three churches is closely linked, each maintains its own identity and separate congregation. The first Colored Primitive Baptist church developed out of a revival held in 1861 and is the largest church in the community. The other two churches were established about fifty years ago by dominant families in other areas of the community. Each had its own pastor. Also founded at this time was a small Missionary Baptist church. The final three churches are affiliated with the holiness-sanctified movement. They are relative newcomers in the community, the earliest having been founded in 1920 and the latest currently in the process of formation.

The proliferation of churches in this small community is based not so much upon differences in religious interpretation as upon the fact of rural isolation and the tendency for small neighborhoods or hamlets to establish their own churches. This is clearly shown in the historical dominance of certain families who occupy positions of authority in the church. On the average, two to three families comprise over half of the membership of any given church, and this network of kin is usually extended bilaterally to include one's uncles, aunts, cousins, nieces, and nephews. In quite rural areas, marriages often occur between the families within a church, thus increasing the solidarity of its members. In instances where marriages take place between members of different churches or denominations, it is common for the husband and wife to retain their previous affiliations and to attend alternatingly one another's churches.

Each church, then, reflects the character of its neighborhood community. The older churches tend to be located in the more rural areas where the traditional ties of land tenure are strong. These churches reflect the affluence and basic security of their members—for example, in terms of size, especially the size and activity of their youth groups. Their services, particularly as indicated by the themes of sermons, stress the traditional elements of personal morality, filial piety, and personal purity. The newer churches tend to be located more centrally in the village; their congregations are made up of recently arrived residents in the community, many coming from areas that were formerly company quarters. These churches are usually smaller than the rural churches; the conduct and content of their services reveal an update of traditional values, embracing such themes as current economic problems and contemporary racism.

The holiness churches constitute an exception to this neighborhood pattern. Membership reflects the predilections of the individual believer and the charismatic appeal of the particular church. Although family orientation is still strong, most of the members—formerly affiliated with the Methodist and Baptist denominations—have chosen to break away from their previous churches in search of a more meaningful religious experience. Generally the holiness churches are smaller than those of the established denominations, and their members less affluent. In the eyes of the community, these people are viewed as different, as malcontents who have turned away from the commonly accepted expression of religious community. The church services are given more to ecstatic expression, and the conduct of the religious life is more strict and puritanical.

Notwithstanding the variations among the different churches, the character of black religiosity transcends specific church affiliation. This is best illustrated in the custom, common in the rural areas of the South, of attending other churches on Sundays when one's own church is not being pastored. At any Sunday service, up to half of those attending are visitors, people who have come to the church either because they have friends there or because the church boasts a dynamic preacher or guest preacher. Thus, there is a distinction between professing religion in general and committing oneself to the membership of a specific church.

To the members of the rural Midway community, the authority of religious conviction lies in feeling. To talk about believing in God is one thing, to "know" him is another—for, as people are fond of repeating, "It is better felt than told."

On one occasion an older woman asked me why I was so intent upon writing everything that she said in my notebook. When I replied that I was interested in learning about religion in the black community, she laughed and said, "You can fill up those notebooks until the day you die, but you will never know God. For if you knew God, you wouldn't be asking all these questions." Humbled, I listened as she related the time in her adolescence when she went to her praying place near the swamp and, in solitude and eager anticipation, was filled by the spirit of the Lord and "got religion." In her words, she was "struck down and shot through to the bone by the quickening light of the Spirit." She has never forgotten that time, for she was "born again of the Spirit," and though she has known suffering, she still awakes every morning calling the name of the Lord.

Religion, then, is something you can "get" at anytime from childhood to old age, though the event usually takes place during adolescence or early adulthood. It can happen in solitude or in a church service, prayer meeting, or revival. The receiving of the Spirit of the Holy Ghost is variously characterized as an experience of anticipation and ecstatic fulfillment. The heartbeat speeds up, the body becomes hot, and one feels a "thirst" within one's body and mind that must be quenched. Then in a moment comes a sense of release like the flight of a bird and one's body and mind become at once trembling and euphorically weightless. This experience may be accompanied by visual appearances which are not to be confused with dream states; as many of the informants stress, the appearance of God is real beyond any doubt. When it happens, the vision is commanding and reduces the individual to a state of fear and trembling.

The following personal history, related by an older woman, may serve as an illustration. Her vision had been experienced soon after the birth of her first child—a particularly difficult period in the woman's life. She had left home with her new husband and was facing poverty in a strange city.

> I first got religion, it occurred in Alabama when I was lying in bed just after my first son was born. I didn't get it in church; I got it all by myself. I was baptized six months later. At this time I prayed to the Lord, and I gave him thanks for giving me a child. I was searching for His understanding. I didn't have much time to do anything else but pray. I wasn't at all frightened. It was a blessing and I have been serving Him ever since. You see, I was a motherless child. I had to take over things when I was very young and I had hard times. So at that time, I asked the Lord to help me with my own children and my brothers and sisters. I came a long way in life without a mother. The Lord called me when I was 23 years old. The Lord had come to me earlier but my mind was not made up until I was older. I didn't have time to stop and pray. When the Lord came to me, I was by myself.

There was nothing to do at that time but turn to the Lord. For the Lord often calls you when you are by yourself. God came to me in a vision. He was wearing a white robe and sandals. He looked like the picture you see in the Bible. The Lord then said to "follow me." We came to some water and I was frightened, because I am scared of water. But God said, "I am the man to save you." So I followed him over the water, and we came to a beautiful white church. When we got to the church, God showed me how to pray.

This experience most often first occurs in solitude. Frequent reference is made to one's "praying place," which may be a bedroom, kitchen, or some secluded spot in the woods. It is a place where one can be "alone with God." The personal, private character of the initial encounter with God's spirit underscores the strongly held belief that communication with God must be personal if it is to be real. In many cases, the actual experience—especially the peak emotional intensity—occurs later in a church service or prayer meeting. In almost all cases, however, the onset of the experience begins with a private feeling or longing.

The personal history of a young man demonstrates the nature of the transition from personal apprehension of the spiritual experience to its public expression. In this instance, the antecedent conditions surrounding the man's life merit noting, because the religious experience frequently takes place during times of great change or crisis in a person's life.

I received God's spirit when I was twenty-six. Before that, I had had some hard times, and most of them were my own fault. I drank a lot and was mean to my wife. Then one day she left with the two children, and when I came home that day the house was empty. Later I found out from neighbors that she had gone to Fort Lauderdale to stay with relatives. I stayed in that house alone, and I didn't want to see anybody. I didn't eat, and I no longer cared for anything in life. I did a lot of thinking, and finally I prayed to God to save my life. The next day I was walking in the area behind my house when suddenly I heard the church bells ring. This was strange because it was noon on a weekday. Then I had a very strange feeling like I was frightened and I began to shake. Quickly, I ran to the church, and when I got there, it was empty. All afternoon I was shaking, because I knew that something was going to happen. That evening I went to a revival which was being held at the church, and went up front to the altar. When the pastor saw me, he knew, and he came and put his hand on my head. At that moment, everything became joy. I can't tell you more. I was unconscious for an hour, and when I came to, everyone was standing around me and praising the Lord.

To "get religion" means to be "born again of the Spirit." One attains a new consciousness, an awareness of being "right on" with God. One is able not only to communicate with God and Christ in prayer, but also to perceive the day-to-day signs and blessings that are seen as omens or guideposts for God's divine plan. Thus, the basic religious experience is a recurrent one, often appearing during times of trial and suffering.

"To be born again" is further an act of cleansing. While religion is something a person only gets once in a lifetime, it can be lost if one does not treasure it. As one informant related:

> Some people get religion, and some don't. I don't really know why. Perhaps some people don't take the time to think of the Lord. You have to make yourself ready for God. Now some people, they get religion but they don't treasure it. The body is the temple of God, just like a church. Now if you let weeds grow around a church, people, they are not going to come. They know that nobody cares about the church. And God, he is not going to come into any unclean place. So God won't come to you if you don't care. The Lord has given you a precious thing; take care to keep it.

Thus the mind and the body, like the church itself, are God's temple and must be kept clean lest God choose not to enter. Having religion entails living a clean life free from the temptations of alcohol, drugs, dancing, and other corruptions of the mind and body. As one informant stated, "You live the simple sweet life."

The interconnecting concepts of "bearing witness" and "praising the Lord" provide a further dimension of religiosity, central to the collective religious expression. Bearing witness is the act of relating to one another's religious experiences, thereby serving as an example of the religious life. To praise the Lord is the joyous expression contained in song, prayer, and responses to sermons. The two are interconnected, insofar as any statement of praise is at the same time a personal statement. When a deacon offers a prayer in a church service, it is in the first analysis a personal testimony of suffering and hope that is fused to the socially shared and symbolically pregnant phraseology of black Christianity. Similarly, the preacher creates in his sermon a sense of drama wherein the historical distance between the present day and biblical times is so minimal that biblical personages become first- and second-person realities in the current lives of the congregation. The sense of drama is well illustrated in the events that occurred during a particular Sunday service. The preacher had just finished serving communion, and had begun his sermon about the Last Supper. He spoke of the suffering of Jesus, the uneasiness of the disciples, and the betrayal by Judas. He also spoke of his own suffering and that of the common man, giving expression to the uncertainties of everyday life and to the betrayal of friends. The tenor of the sermon then became more emotional, and the preacher broke into a rhythmic style, gasping out short and intensely personal statements. "I saw the suffering of my Lord! I felt the betrayal of Judas! I didn't know where to turn!" As he became more personal, the congregation joined in with soulful humming and shouts of "Amen," "Right on," and "Thank you, Jesus." Then the congregation became ecstatic, shouting and thanking Jesus.

The church, like the mind and body of the individual, is the temple of God. If the mood of the singing, the prayers, and the sermon are "right on," and if everyone's mind is in accord, God is seen as sending down his Holy Ghost to the congregation. The Spirit then moves from "heart to heart" and spiritually unites the people like a current of electricity. It is the achievement of this emotional tenor that constitutes the single criterion of a successful service, for not only does it "prove" once again the presence of God, but it also reinforces in the people's minds their own existence as a successful spiritual community.

Meanwhile, outside the doors of the church lurks the Devil, seeking to sow the seeds of dissension and to separate the unwary sheep from the flock. While the church service may achieve a spiritual tone where the Devil dares not enter, the people must leave this spiritual ambiance and return to their daily lives. Thus, the spiritual rejuvenation or purification attained in the church service is subject to corruption, and the Devil, who hides in the unknown recesses of our minds, is always ready to corrupt.

The Devil is as real as the Spirit of God, and both may be seen as struggling for control of man's mind and thus his destiny. The Devil is variously conceived as a voice in one's conscience that reveals itself in temptation. Drinking, dancing, lust, and other temptations of the flesh are the work of the Devil. Such temptations are commonly seen as beyond the conscious control of the individual because the Devil is tricky and devious. He enters our minds when we least expect it; and before we know it, we are in a struggle with him.

The following describes one man's periodic encounter with the Devil. The man, whom I shall call Pete, is about sixty years old, illiterate, and employed as an unskilled laborer. His experience with the Devil is closely tied to his drinking problem. Most often this experience would occur on a Friday evening after work, and begin with feelings of nervous agitation, bad temper, and withdrawal. These feelings then would focus upon an obsessive compulsion for alcohol. There was nothing that could restrain him, and all the time he was drinking he knew that he would suffer later. Yet it felt good and eased the pain and tension in his body. That night in bed he would lie awake and toss in a kind of impotent rage. It was then he knew that the Devil had him, and the more he struggled, the more he saw the Devil cruelly laughing at his misery. The next morning he would awaken in depression and disgust, and to relieve the pain, he would begin drinking again, all the time falling more and more into the hands of the Devil. As Pete said, "All the Devil wants is to kill you, and you are a fool because you let him do it." Finally with fear and trembling, Pete would put down the bottle and take to bed; after hours of inner struggle, he would "cast the Devil off his back," whereupon he would feel a renewed vigor and sense of life.

Such interpretations of personal experience may be seen repeatedly in cases involving alcoholism, sexual licentiousness, vengeance, and other states of compulsive passion. The initial feeling of stress gives way to compulsion, which in turn gives way to temporary stress reduction. Yet, unlike the religious experience of God's spirit, the sensed euphoria is always followed by further suffering, self-degradation, and retribution. Alcoholism brings with it a hangover and d.t.'s; explosive lasciviousness and violence typically result in a more hostile and dangerous situation.

While the Devil is regarded as the cause of suffering, he is often perceived with a paradoxical sense of humor and admiration. The content and mood of this perception are well illustrated in an interview with a local black minister. The minister related with humor God's confrontation with Satan in the Garden of Eden.

> You know, that old Satan beat God. He made Eve eat the apple. God was angry but He couldn't do a thing. That's the way the Devil is. He's tricky and he can sneak up on you when God's not looking. God made that Devil to tempt folks. For He said to the Devil that man would beat him on the head but that the Devil would always be grabbing his heel. [See Genesis 3:15.] That's like the Devil, you know. Man goes through life and thinks everything is fine. Then just when you don't expect it, up jumps the Devil and he trips you.

This paradoxical attitude toward the Devil is found in countless secular connotations. In popular usage, a person of moody and violent disposition is said to have "the Devil in him." Even an ornery pig or cow may be thought of jokingly as so possessed. The Devil also signifies a "bad nigger" or "bad ass mother-fucker." Thus a person who is callous, manipulative, and clever may be admired as a Devil. Finally, the white man—or certain white people—are often hostilely referred to as "white devils."

While God offers inner peace and purpose, the Devil is the brute force of fragmentary purpose in the guise of a taste of honey. From a psychological standpoint, the Devil is that inner compulsion that contravenes one's better "instincts," or rationality, and drives one to self-destruction. Yet the Devil is not necessarily considered evil—at least not in the southern white fundamentalist sense of the concept. Instead, he is an everyday fact of life; and when a black says, "The Devil is going to get you," the sentiment is more one of cautious advice than fear of contamination or damnation. The Devil best approximates a kind of cynical reality principle that tells it like it is—tells us how bad it is and how bad he is. When we agree, when we succumb, that old Devil just sits back and laughs—because that is reality. The Devil is just "one bad nigger."

God and Devil—good and evil—are not always simple propositions, especially for black people whose historical experience has been twisted between the oppression and sham of white moral justice and the perceived sense of individual and collective inadequacy. Black religion places little emphasis upon moral purity or upon a hard-and-fast distinction between the saved and the damned. In black sermons, there are few references to hell and damnation; the man who has drunk, stolen, cursed, and thus engaged the Devil, can nonetheless thank God that he has religion. Blacks go to church to "praise God," and praising God is fun whether one is pious or a sinner.

This absence of distinction stands in marked contrast to my perception of southern white Protestantism. As Samuel Hill (1972) notes, the white Southerner places great emphasis upon the purity of private morality, which he sees as the source of the genius underlying his social order. The white Southerner's concept of God is profoundly moral. Hill (1972:34) writes: "He has standards, is altogether holy, cannot countenance evil, sends his son to pay the sin-debt, and requires total loyalty. Accordingly, man is defined as moral: one who by Adam's choice is alienated, can decide, must decide and is capable of considerable spiritual attainment." This entails "getting right with God," making the right decisions, and practicing what one preaches. To fail to exercise control over behavior, even for a moment, threatens a person's spiritual status—his place before the throne of God.

A religion that rigidly adheres to purity produces an equally intense concept of impurity. The white view of the Devil is similar to that of blacks: he is the source of worldly temptation that pulls people away from a true relationship with God. The difference, however, is that the white conceptualization is deeply tied to the idea of sin. Salvation is the forgiveness of sin, the washing away of impurity. The Devil is the embodiment of evil, the defiler of one's spiritual status.

In her discussion of the concept of purity, Mary Douglas (1966:194) suggests a comparative framework for the analysis of cultural world views based upon their acceptance or rejection of evil. The former, which she terms "dirt-affirming," existentially accepts evil without stigma or fear of contamination. The latter, or "dirt-rejecting," philosophy is rigid and fixed, erecting strong moral dichotomies and passionately rejecting evil as the source of spiritual damnation. The parallel between Douglas's dichotomy and that which exists between blacks and whites is readily apparent. Midway blacks see evil—and hence the Devil—as manifest everywhere in the real world; and human existence provides little occasion for moral piety or pretense. Salvation, or the union of people with God's spirit, is not so much a release from sin as a release from suffering in a world that is inherently sinful. The southern black world view is, therefore, dirt-affirming, and exists in polar contrast to the dirt-rejecting philosophy of the white Southerner.

An explanation of these differences requires examination of the differences in ethnic and religious heritage, and of the historical tradition of racism with its institutional and ideological opposition of blacks and whites. A full discussion of these causes is beyond the scope of this paper; space permits but few observations.

Scholars such as Herskovits (1958) and Blassingame (1972) have argued that the institution of slavery created and maintained conditions of cultural segregation that required the autonomy of blacks and preserved much of their ethnic heritage, especially in the area of religious expression. The emphasis upon rhythm in song, prayer, and sermonic exhortation points to a retention of particularly affective and dramatic styles of West African tradition. With respect to the question of God and Devil, the West African world view lacks any concept akin to the moralistic dichotomies of the Judaeo-Christian tradition, much less the Euro-American Protestant idea of personal piety and individual salvation. As Mbiti (1969) argues, good and evil—purity and sin—are seen by Africans as the existential conditions of being in the world. It is human actions vis-à-vis the spiritual world that determine the relative presence of good and evil. If a person chooses to behave by the moral axioms of custom, he is then in harmony with God, and the conditions of his life become prosperous and good. If he chooses to be ruled by antisocial passions, then he is in disequilibrium with the spiritual world, and his life will be filled with suffering and affliction.

The opposition between good and evil is very well characterized by the trickster figure in West African mythology. The trickster, most often represented as a spider or rabbit, is typically small, somewhat ludicrous or foolish in deportment, but extremely clever. In myths and tales, he is seen as confronting challenges through devious means and manipulating people in authority to promote his own welfare. As I have argued elsewhere (Grindal 1973), the meaning of the trickster is the rebellion against authority—a psychological escape valve for the tensions created by the strong requirements of a socially intense and authoritarian moral order. Symbolically the trickster represents an ironic affirmation of evil—the victory of the individual over authority. It is not surprising, then, to find that this mythological figure of the trickster has come to be symbolically associated with the Devil.

As Blassingame (1972) argues, the major thrust of slave religion was the attainment of power for collective self-determination. The amoral characterization of the trickster embodies these values of rebellion. In the African context, the values served to counter the highly authoritarian and collective tendency of traditional society. Under slavery they intensified in a context of absolute social and ideological inequality. Ironically, Christianity, which promises salvation, ultimate dignity, and freedom, is fused to a secular existence lacking any such promise. Thus, the principal tenet of the religion is escape from bondage. In slave times, as now, the theme of "going home," of escaping the bonds of suffering, is juxtaposed upon the dimensions of good and evil. Bondage is an existential condition of cultural alienation both in the everyday realm of social interaction and in the deepest religious conceptualization.

Given the inherently universal and humanistic tenets of Christianity, its co-existence with racism necessarily meant that black people were stripped of their humanity. Only in such a way could the "morality" of racism be dismissed as spiritually insignificant, thereby permitting the personal salvation of whites. The ideological rationalizations are many. The myth of the morally righteous slave owner, discussed at length by Cash (1941), fostered a paternalistic view of white superiority and the childlike, uncivilized nature of blacks. The justifications for black inferiority abound with biblical reference: the mark of Cain, the descendants of Ham, and even the serpent in the Garden. The idea that the black is a sinner against God who has been humbled to servitude for his pride and vanity is well taken in the autobiographical accounts of many black writers. Such a view on the part of blacks represents at least a partial acceptance of the white world view and an awareness of the fundamental differences in blacks' racial identities and relative positions in the social order. Walter White (1948) described how, in an encounter with a lynch mob in Atlanta, he was suddenly gripped by the knowledge of his racial identity as one marked for expulsion or extinction, as one who has been on the losing side of every historical battle and cosmic struggle.

Religious inferiority speaks to the question of alienation. To be damned, to be naturally born as a misfit destined as a slave, is to experience profound alienation. Being black gives to existence a certain destiny that expresses the futility of escape. Although one can escape poverty through fortune or achievement, blackness is inescapable. To be black in the rural South meant—and still often means—to exist in a castelike structure that denies legitimate access to the goods and just rewards of southern life. Blacks, thus damned, are alien to the white secular moral order and, in the ultimate racist interpretation, are excluded from the ranks of the saved.

For blacks, evil is a basic quality of the human experience; it stems from the ideological perception that the world was not made equally. The separation of black and white is ultimately a question of oppression, which for blacks is the cause of evil and suffering. Yet the cause of oppression, and hence of black people's position in the social order, is not one of their own making. Clearly they are not responsible for their bondage. If the black is damned, it is because the world itself is evil. The attainment of salvation, therefore, is not so much a question of morality as it is an escape from one's existential bondage.

The religiosity of blacks does not accept the premise of nihilism: on the contrary, its precise thrust is the attainment of spiritual freedom. This is achieved both by the temporary attainment of religious ecstasy and by the release of death and the promise of ultimate fulfillment in heaven. The spirit of God is the freedom from the suffering of this world. Ironically, then, the black world view, while affirming the existence of evil, is able to transcend it, and maintain a religious potential of great purity, force, and vision.

REFERENCES

Blassingame, John W., 1972. *The Slave Community* (New York: Oxford University Press).

Cash, W. J., 1941. *The Mind of the South* (New York: Vintage Books).

Douglas, Mary, 1966. *Purity and Danger* (London: Routledge and Kegan Paul).

Gearhart, Edward B., 1956. St. Paul's Church in Quincy, Florida, during the Territorial Period. *Florida Historical Quarterly* 34:339–65.

Grindal, Bruce T., 1973. The Sisala Trickster Tale. *Journal of American Folklore* 86:173–74.

Herskovits, Melville J., 1958. *The Myth of the Negro Past* (Boston: Beacon Press).

Hill, Samuel S., 1972. The South's Two Cultures. In *Religion in the Solid South*, Samuel S. Hill, ed. (Nashville: Abingdon Press), pp. 24–26.

Mbiti, John S., 1969. *African Religions and Philosophy* (New York: Praeger).

Richardson, Joe M., 1963. *The Negro in the Reconstruction of Florida* (Ph.D. diss., Florida State University).

White, Walter, 1948. *A Man Called White* (New York: Viking Press).

Language, Vision, Myth:
The Primitive Baptist Experience of Grace

BRETT SUTTON

Whenever Christian belief places the individual at the operative center of the process of salvation, personal testimony assumes special significance, both for the believer and for the historian. Personal accounts of religious experience serve as a valuable supplement to the theoretical and exegetical writings on which our understanding of Christian history depends. The paradigm of the form is Augustine's *Confessions*, in which the author demonstrated in a profound way how his own personal life history was the proving ground of grace. But not until after the Reformation—when the old hierarchy of priestly mediation between believer and deity was displaced by an unmediated dialogue between individual and God—did published personal religious narratives become numerous enough to constitute a genre. It was the impulse for introspection among Puritans and Quakers, in fact, that gave colonial America one of her first important literary forms, the spiritual autobiography (Shea 1968). That tradition has persisted. The written memoirs and personal accounts by the American heirs of British nonconformism, from the journal of John Winthrop to the autobiography of Oral Roberts, comprise an album of American Christian self-portraits of great historical value. For all their many differences, these works share the notion that the revealed word of God is inscribed in one's own heart as well as in the pages of the Bible.

From an ethnological point of view, however, these writings present a serious limitation: they are largely the work of church leaders, the spokesmen for their faiths who might be expected to be more reflective, theological, and didactic than the average churchgoer, and thus tend to reveal more of the formal orthodoxy than the religion as believed and practiced. Rarely do we have access to a more broadly based kind of personal narrative: the anecdotal, informal, orally presented personal experiences of common church folk (see, for example, Johnson 1969). Such testimonies are more likely to be delivered spontaneously to an assembly of fellow believers than to be composed in the solitude of the study, and are thus lost to history unless interested students seek them out and record them. This essay presents in brief a collection of such narratives, gathered among a group of black Primitive Baptists in the southeastern United States in 1979.[1] My purpose is to demonstrate their utility in the study of religion.

The Primitive Baptists, found today in many parts of the country but in high concentrations in the rural South, are among a small group of American churches that survived the nineteenth century with their Calvinism intact: they still hold to doctrines long abandoned by both evangelical and liberal Christians. For the Primitive Baptists, the end of the world was foreordained from the beginning—the saved will be called to grace by God at a time of his own choosing, and the condemned are irretrievably lost. Therefore, there is no effort on their part to baptize children, to conduct Sunday schools, to establish missions, or to participate generally in the evangelization of the world. To do so would not only be a waste of time; according to predestinarian theology, it also would be arrogant and self-deceiving, because God's power is sufficient and his plan is not contingent upon human action. The church's stiff-necked resistance to what it regards as liberal encroachments has not always attracted large congregations or fostered congenial relationships with neighboring denominations. The Primitive Baptists, however, seem quite comfortable in their role as a "peculiar" people and take some pride in their reputation for not cooperating with "the world."

The words that Primitive Baptists use to describe their encounters with God may take the form of reports of healing experiences, personal interpretations of theological points, exemplary stories, or accounts of natural phenomena in which the hand of God is evident. But the verbalizations of greatest interest to me here are the narrative accounts of personal experiences of grace, dream-like visions that descend upon an individual in moments of solitude or during sleep. These visions constitute a fundamental source of religious inspiration for the members of the church. The believer's close personal relationship with God, which is a central Protestant theme, thus assumes special importance among the Primitive Baptists. More than mere inspiration, the visionary experience is the foundation of the believer's petition for admission to the church: it is an independent verification that the candidate has come, not of his own will, but in obedience to a divine call. Several generations ago the report of a miraculous experience of grace was mandatory—church membership was closed to all who could not recount an appropriate spiritual experience. Although official policy has softened in recent years and more generalized expressions of commitment to the church are now acceptable as demonstrations of sincerity, the old-style experience remains highly valued and is frequently reported, both by new converts and by long-time members.

The form that these narratives take is particularly significant. They are not simply emotional responses to the moment of grace, nor are they conveyed in the language of interpretive theology. They are, instead, highly personalized sacred stories, vivid, richly detailed descriptions of supernatural events in which the subject himself is an actor. They are narrative rather than expository, constituted more of drama than affect, and they consist of a complex sequence of interrelated structural elements. The distinguishing characteristics of these narratives of religious experience are easily illustrated using contrasting excerpts—one set from the published personal histories of three well-known Christian leaders, the other from conversations with black Primitive Baptists.

The first passage comes from the journal of the English Methodist John Wesley. The entry is for May 24, 1738, the date of his conversion: "In the evening I went very unwillingly to a society in Aldersgate Street, where one was reading Luther's preface to the Epistle to the Romans. About a quarter before nine, while he was describing the change which God works in the heart through faith in Christ, I felt my heart strangely warmed. I felt I did trust in Christ, Christ alone for my salvation, and an assurance was given me that He had taken away *my* sins, even *mine*, and saved *me* from the law of sin and death" (Wesley 1938:475–76).

The next excerpt is from the *Memoirs* of Charles G. Finney, a prominent Presbyterian evangelist of the nineteenth century: "Just at that point a passage of scripture seemed to drop into my mind with a flood of light. . . . I instantly seized hold of this with my heart. I had intellectually believed in the Bible before, but never had the truth been in my mind that faith was a voluntary trust instead of an intellectual state. . . . I knew that it was God's work, and God's voice, as it were, that spoke to me" (Finney 1973:16).

Finally, here is part of the conversion experience of Dwight L. Moody, an early promoter of the YMCA and a successful businessman-evangelist, as cited in his biography: "I thought the old sun shone brighter than it ever had before. I thought it was just smiling on me. As I walked up the Boston Common and heard the birds singing in the trees, I thought they were all singing a song to me" (William R. Moody 1931:35).

A particularly striking feature of these excerpts is that they deal almost exclusively with subjective emotional states. Each is a thoughtful contemplation of relatively vague feelings in the heart of the narrator. Without question, some kind of datable event has taken place, but the core of that event—however rich it may be with subjective meaning—lacks the physical reality of events in the everyday world. The essential component of each passage is not something observable, even by the internal spiritual eye of the narrator, but is instead the individual's *perception* of his own spiritual state. The narrator's presence is strong but serves in an interpretive rather than in a participatory capacity. Wesley's phrase "I felt my heart strangely warmed" comes closest to describing a palpable event. For the most part, the language is seasoned with qualifiers that place the narratives on the side of thought rather than experience. Finney's "seemed to drop" and "as it were," and Moody's "I thought," are unimportant syntactically, but crucial semantically, indicating that at root the experience lacks objective reality.

Here, by contrast, are excerpts from informal interviews that I conducted with three Primitive Baptists.[2] Each is only a portion of a longer visionary experience. The first is from a vision that the elderly speaker had had relatively recently: "God placed me on a white horse. And this horse was faster than lightning. I was afraid. The horse was travelling so fast you couldn't hear the feet when they touched the ground. Anybody ever rode a fast horse, they know you lean, the horse go which way you lean. This horse didn't turn to the right or to the left. He went through buildings, I was still riding him. Come a large tree. I tried to lean the horse around the tree, but he went straight through. Let me know, don't you turn to the right; don't you turn to the left."

The second excerpt is part of the experience which encouraged the speaker to claim the calling of a minister: "I was sitting between my father and an old elder in a church that was full of people. And when I saw myself get up to preach, I saw I had a golden trumpet in my hands, and I placed it up to my mouth. I blew through that trumpet, and music came out, and you could see it. And it went out to the people, and they reached out and ate that music."

The narrator of the third excerpt is a particularly gifted man who has been the subject of dozens of visionary experiences over the course of his life: "And a lot of people were mingling out there. They was just out there, just rolling and a-talking and a-carrying on. And I was standing over there to myself. And I was standing, look like to me, about that height, about 30 inches off the ground. And I didn't see no track, nothing of the kind. There was a mountain back toward the east, and it was a valley, a cutaway that come between them two mountains. I couldn't see round the curve. But I was looking in that direction for the little train to come. I thought it was gonna be a big train. I didn't know it was gonna be a little train. And it was coming, a little white train about that big, wasn't hardly big as two inches, coming around the curve there. Didn't have too many coaches behind it. And it was pretty as a doll. White as snow. Didn't be moving on no track, but sailing through the air. And it come right up to me."

Clearly these narratives differ in kind from the written expositions. In the written accounts, the interpretive, analytic, and emotional content is high; but in the Primitive Baptist experiences, the emphasis is on the dramatic, the narrative, and the concrete. The organizing element in the first set of examples, the interpretive presence of the speaker, is virtually absent in the latter narratives; in its place stands a sequence of events—a plot. Technically, the diction in the Primitive Baptist narratives is in the first person, but the narrative voice is rather more journalistic than personal, more objective than interpretive, focusing on events rather than feelings. The statements give the impression that anyone else who happened to be there when the event occurred would have described it in nearly the same terms. The narratives are linguistically framed so that, from the speaker's point of view, the locus of the event is external to the individual who witnesses it. In some ways, the closest counterparts of the Primitive Baptist narratives are not the published testimonies of American evangelicals, but the accounts of miracles in the Roman Catholic church, or the miraculous providences recorded by American Puritans. One difference, however, is that the Primitive Baptist dramas occur in private spiritual places, unapproachable by any other mortal.

The visionary experience becomes social reality only in its narrative form. As pure experience, the encounter with the Spirit is an event to which neither one's fellow church members nor outside investigators have direct access. If it is to be consummated, it must be presented publicly in an appropriate verbal form. Because the report of the vision is oral, rather than written, it cannot exist independent of its telling; it is irreducibly a process of communication requiring the simultaneous participation of both speaker and audience. Narration is the key moment in the transformation of a personal event into a communal one, a transformation in which language is the catalyst.

Public speaking and rhetorical skill are highly valued by the members of these Primitive Baptist churches, and there is admirable craft in the best testimonies, sermons, and prayers. There is, in fact, a commonly held understanding that words spoken spontaneously are gifts of the Spirit, expressing a higher order of truth than words written down on paper. Preachers, for example, believe that only the Spirit can grant eloquence, and they will not so much as prepare notes for their sermons. They have, in fact, considerable disdain for those seminary-educated ministers whose oratorical gifts are so poor that they must write out their sermons in advance. Members feel the same way about their personal visionary experiences, taking a measure of pride in the fact that they do not have to plan what to say, and relishing the spiritual excitement that runs through the congregation as a vision is re-created verbally for the general blessing of all. For Primitive Baptists, as for Durkheim, the solitary believer is an anomaly.

The narratives do not always take exactly the same form, but are appropriate to their contexts. For example, stories exchanged among several friends standing outside the church before the service tend to be condensed and conversational. The description of a vision given to an outsider, such as those given me in the course of interviews, is detailed and interspersed with supplementary explanations of theological points that the listener would be unlikely to know. A vision narrative that is woven into a sermon becomes oral poetry—formulaic, low in denotative language, rich in description, and expressed as a metrical, melodic chant.

Each visionary experience is unique and nonrepeatable. It can neither be solicited from God nor shared directly with others. Its values lies precisely in the fact that it is a personalized message from God to a single individual, one that speaks to the recipient's own needs and background. However, when a number of narratives are gathered together, written out, and examined as artifacts, clear symbolic and structural patterns emerge. It could be said, with some justification, that collectively the stories constitute a body of oral literature.

The term *literature* deserves some comment. Northrop Frye (1957:74) notes that true literature does not attempt to match real events with a verbal structure, but that its meaning is hypothetical—"not true, not false"—a form of expression where questions of fact are "subordinated to the primary aim of producing a structure of words for its own sake." In Frye's terms, the Primitive Baptist vision narratives are assertive rather than literary, since, from the speaker's point of view, they are neither autonomous nor imaginative, but attempt to describe accurately a real event—the visionary experience. Frye's distinction is useful and has considerable explanatory power in the context of mainstream Western literary tradition. However, in the cross-cultural ethnographic context, particularly where religious belief is involved, the distinction between the imaginative and the factual becomes problematic. True, vision narratives purport to describe "real" events; equally true, the reality of those events cannot be independently verified nor the verbal descriptions evaluated for accuracy as in the case of true assertive narratives.

It is unrewarding, it seems, to classify these narratives solely on the basis of an elusive facticity that cannot be determined by the usual means. Indeed, from the less ambiguous point of view of function and form, the narratives look very much like literary products: they are rich in metaphor, narrators deliver them with poetic craft, and listeners—especially outsiders—appreciate them as verbal performances "for their own sake" as well as accounts of true spiritual events. In short, the narratives may not be fictive at root, but at the social level they function, in part, as literature. We may thus explore the images of the narratives as "symbols" in a literary sense, even though to the narrators they represent only themselves. It is precisely this distinction that allows anthropologists to consider the literary features of myths and religious poetry separately from questions of belief. Another literary critic has recognized similar strong fictional overtones in the work of the spiritual autobiographer: "Reading his work may provide the same imaginative complexities as experiencing a novel; the presumed difference in authorial intent between fictional and factual records makes little necessary difference in effect, though it poses knotty philosophic and literary questions" (Spacks 1976:39).

A complete description of the symbolic elements that appear regularly in these stories is beyond the scope of this essay, but a few summarizing remarks are in order. Many of the dominant images in the narratives echo important biblical symbols. For example, the golden trumpet of the second excerpt is akin to various trumpets of power in the Scriptures, from those of Joshua at Jericho to the seven trumpets of doom in Revelation. Another example is the frequent location of visionary events on or near mountain peaks, the setting where the prophets retired to speak with God and the site of a number of important events in the life of Christ. Also, the narratives contain numerous visionary descriptions of spiritual beings and the Holy City itself that repeat the images and even the exact language of the King James Bible. Other references in the narratives are not specifically biblical, but express values rooted in Western culture and the English language. For example, whiteness often expresses divine purity; children, innocence; storms and wild beasts, danger and chaos. Still other images are products of American vernacular Christianity. The little white train in the third excerpt is only one of many products of modern technology that play expressive roles in the narratives. Such figures are ubiquitous in southern folk religion, and include not only trains, but automobiles, telephones, and radios.

No folk literature is purely collective, of course. However rich the shared stock of images may be, it is the individual narrator, or re-creator, who gives final form to the story. This is particularly true in the Primitive Baptist visionary mode, where the emphasis is on individual revelation and the uniqueness of each incident. Personal motifs, such as features of the local landscape, friends of the narrator, and significant aspects of his own life, take their places in these narratives in unpredictable ways. It is only within the personal framework that the central symbols are able to operate; the tradition only furnishes building blocks, not completed stories. One of the most interesting features of the visionary process is its ability to join public and private images and thus to produce a seamless narrative that is meaningful in both a general and a personal sense.

The similarities among the narratives are structural as well as symbolic. One structural pattern in particular occurs frequently, and may in fact be a kind of generative model. The pattern can be summarized as follows: As the vision begins, the subject moves from a condition of ordinary reality into a special visionary state of pervasive gloom, mystery, or danger. Having crossed over a boundary into a world where spiritual reality displaces nature, the subject either witnesses or participates in miraculous events, and suffers an ordeal that both threatens and transforms him. Typical patterns include death followed by miraculous revival, a successful struggle to cross a nearly insurmountable barrier with the help of a divine agent, and a long and awesome journey in the company of a spiritual being. In the end, the subject is released from the control of divine power and returns to the world, scared and sobered, but rejuvenated. This model is familiar to anthropologists, for it is the classic ritual structure of separation/margin/aggregation articulated by Van Gennep (1960) at the turn of the century and extended analytically by Turner (1969).

The narratives, it must be pointed out, do not always manifest the complete structure. For one thing, a complete visionary experience may express only a portion of the structure. For another, in certain social contexts, the narrator may not recount the entire event as he perceived it. This is particularly true of preachers, who use only that part of the story that suits their rhetorical purposes. Since the members of the congregation have had similar experiences themselves and fully understand the dynamics of the genre, a partial or condensed narrative may convey to the listeners the burden of the complete story. When a preacher says, "God came into my room that morning and took out my hard and stoney heart," he is not necessarily using a figure of speech, but may in fact be alluding to an actual visionary event.

Without dwelling upon the ambiguities of genre theory or the confusion introduced by the definition of terms, I would like to suggest that vision narratives, as oral literature, are akin to myths in several ways. This is not to say, of course, that they share all of the features usually associated with myths: they rarely survive intact over several generations, and they are never etiological, to name two exceptions. My purpose is not to categorize, but to highlight certain features of the narratives by comparing them with a standard narrative category.

It is typical of myths that they relate the experiences of deities, or at least of ancestors and heroes of superhuman or supernatural stature. This is also true of the Primitive Baptist narratives: the personages and animals that appear in them are not of the profane world, but are classified by the narrators themselves as spiritual beings. The stories are also sacred in the more general sense that they describe the dramatic penetration of sacred "reality" into the "real" world of the recipient, and thus the suspension of natural law. The Primitive Baptists, despite their name, do not exhibit the prelogical inability to distinguish between the real and the magical, which Lévy-Bruhl (1926) falsely attributed to "primitive" peoples. Rather, it is precisely the believer's solid grounding in the logic of the natural world that gives the visions significance as spiritual suspensions of that reality.

If the vision itself is the penetration of the real by the spiritual, then the narrative description of the vision is an indirect manifestation of the same thing. Since the original event can never be experienced again, the secondary, narrative version becomes primary; it is the only durable and tangible form that the experience can take—its only means of survival in the social world. This is characteristic of all myths that thrive in a religious oral tradition. Mircea Eliade points out, "By reciting the myths one reconstitutes that fabulous time and hence in some sort becomes 'contemporary' with the events described, one is in the presence of the Gods or Heroes" (1963:18). The principal difference is that, for the Primitive Baptists, the "fabulous time" reconstituted in the narrative is personal rather than collective, and recent rather than remote.

From this analytical perspective the Bible is also mythical. The printed text successfully formalizes and stabilizes the biblical cycle of myths in a form well suited to the needs of a literate society. However, for the Primitive Baptists, whose visionary experiences overlap thematically and symbolically with Scripture, biblical and experiential truth are two points on a single continuum, and there is no significant difference in source or authority. Institutionalized and personalized myths are complementary. The difference between the visions of the Old Testament prophets, expressed as Scripture, and those of individual church members, expressed as narrative, is one of degree, not kind. Primitive Baptists generally tend to reduce the written and the revealed word to the same order of reality. For example, members believe that the printed words of the Bible are dead and meaningless until God awakens in the reader the spirit of understanding, just as one's life lacks meaning until God awakens it with a visionary experience. It is significant, too, that preachers and lay members alike frequently quote and paraphrase the Bible without benefit of printed text, granting the Scriptures, in effect, a narrative vitality similar to that of the vision accounts.

Another common observation about myth is that it validates ritual, providing a cognitive context in which the participants may act with security and confidence. Examination of the various forms of collective ritual in the Primitive Baptist church does not reveal actions that are subject to direct validation by the radically individualistic visionary experience. Yet the vision is powerful as a validatory force of a different sort, producing a sense of security in the individual that is manifested in his original petition to join the church, in the various sorts of ceremonial public narrations of the vision, and, less directly, in the individual's confident participation in the whole range of church ritual. In structure, there are differences between this personal vision/action relationship and the more public myth/ritual relationship, but functionally they are similar, to the extent that the personal experience is the validation of the believer's presence among the elect.

As I mentioned above, one feature of these narratives that sets them apart from myths is that they do not become disconnected from their original sources. One theory concerning the origins of myths holds that the personal dreams of a particular individual, because of his social status, the content of the dreams, and historical conditions, become canonized through retelling. They eventually lose contact with their source and, in time, attain the durability and status of myth. It is a plausible explanation, albeit difficult to prove, since the history of certain nativistic movements, such as the Native American ghost dance and the Melanesian cargo cults, lends support to the idea. Primitive Baptist visions do, in fact, appear frequently in the form of dreams, although members insist that they can always tell the difference. But the chance that the personal vision of a single church member will cross over into the public domain is extremely small. Several factors, including the regular flow of new vision accounts into the group, the Primitive Baptist sense of radical individualism, and the overshadowing presence of the paradigmatic revelation of the Bible, combine in the Primitive Baptist community to confine visions to their personal forms.

The Primitive Baptists have no monopoly on visionary experiences. Similar narratives can be found in other Christian denominations and among other cultural groups. Since religious belief is systematic, it is always profitable to inquire into the reasons for the presence of religious phenomena, and the question here is this: why have vision narratives taken root as a stable form among Primitive Baptists in particular? The inquiry in this case leads to the complexities of predestinarian theology.

Crucial here is the problem of assurance: assurance that the doctrines in which one believes are unequivocally true and, therefore, that one's participation in actions predicated on these doctrines is legitimate. The problem confronts all religious people in some form, but it is a particularly significant problem for Christians who claim for themselves the New Birth, because the change is not always verified by unambiguous proof. In Protestant theology, the believer's choices are polarized—one is either saved or one is not—and the trick is to establish to one's own satisfaction on which side of the dividing line one stands. American evangelicals have had to confront this problem repeatedly, for their freewill theology displaced the older Calvinistic determinism, leaving salvation standing on a shaky new foundation of human choice. In a freewill system, where salvation is available to all, assurance is almost too easily had. For many observers, including Primitive Baptists, the ecstasies and excesses of protracted meetings and revivals are dangerous because they may hypnotize worshipers into taking their emotional responses in the heat of the service as signs of genuine religious conversion, when in fact the responses may have only been elicited by what one moderate Presbyterian called the "sport of lesser passions" (Boles 1972:96). It is a problem in practice as well as in theory: too often, a soul carried into the church by emotional zeal slips quickly back to the devil as the heat of the revival dissipates. Not every spiritual emotion signifies conversion.

In one sense, the Primitive Baptists have avoided the problem of assurance by repudiating any ability to influence their own salvation. There is no need to worry about the legitimacy of one's voluntary acts of religious expression if all voluntary acts are defined as being "of man" and therefore spiritually worthless. Any confirmation of salvation that is known to arise within the individual is immediately suspect because a soul submerged in sin is incapable of extracting itself. The task for each Primitive Baptist, then, is not that of sifting through his motivations to find one that sanctions his own decision, but that of discovering what decision was made in his behalf "before the foundation of the world." The believer cannot act, but must wait—sometimes for an oppressively long time—to be acted *upon* by a transforming experience that is so clearly external to the self that it is trustworthy. In effect, the stronger the believer's desire for salvation, the more untrustworthy are his personal convictions.

Into the midst of the believer's quandary comes the powerful, spontaneous, dramatic encounter with the Spirit, bestowing freedom and confidence. Anything less is subject to doubt born of the fallibility of human choice. The vision, so clearly external to the individual and beyond the reach of his will, constitutes a mythical rather than a conceptual experience of God and creates in the convert the assurance that he is truly chosen. More specifically, it spares him the agonizing prospect of living with a less than dependable choice and of facing the paradox of infinite regress, of choosing whether or not to choose. For the Primitive Baptists, and perhaps for any Christian who experiences grace in visionary form, it is not necessary to purchase salvation with the devalued currency of self-conscious choice. This may be why Primitive Baptists do not use the popular fundamentalist phrase "*get* saved," with its grammatical suggestion of manipulative taking. It may also explain why, in contrast to some members of other denominations, they claim to feel less responsibility for becoming church members and more security in their membership. As one member put it, "I can join the church, and I can unjoin, but if the Lord join me to it, then I'll stay there."

Stated another way, the problem of the believer is an unfortunate by-product of Cartesian dualism, in which the mind contemplates its own salvation as an object. When salvation becomes subject to volition, the will attains a kind of independence and becomes the adversary of temptation. But the autonomous will, though it may successfully lift itself by its own spiritual bootstraps, falls vulnerable to the hazards of arrogant perfectionism and overconfidence, which risks the sin of pride, and backsliding, which threatens the will's claim to power. There are various theological solutions to this dilemma. For the Primitive Baptists, the remedy seems to be rooted in predestinarianism and visionary experience: the former establishes cognitively the limits of the will; the latter demonstrates it. The visionary experience induces nothing less than the subordination of the self, including the will, to a higher power, dislodging even the most deeply entrenched feelings of personal autonomy. What the quest for salvation has divided, the visionary experience reassembles. Of course, doubt and self-consciousness are not forever banished by the vision. The postvisionary return to human imperfection inevitably weakens the believer's sensation of grace and may even rekindle old feelings of personal inadequacy. But faced with that, the believer does not exert the will with renewed energy, but simply awaits faithfully the return of the Spirit. The visionary experience gives release, not from the pain of mortality, but from the treadmill of willing and doubt.

The spiritual freedom attained by Primitive Baptists has been described in broader philosophical terms by phenomenologist Paul Ricoeur. In order to release itself from the bondage of the will, "the Ego must more radically renounce the covert claim of all consciousness, must abandon its will to posit itself, so that it can receive the nourishing and inspiring spontaneity which breaks the sterile circle of the self's constant return to self" (1966:14).

For Primitive Baptists, the visionary experience is the catalytic event that severs the mind's closed loop of obsessive questing and self-consciousness, and dissolves the paradox that the sinner, sunken in a state of wretchedness and alienation from God, must himself begin the transformation that secures freedom from that state. The visions are often terrifying, but out of the terror and loss of self emerges an assurance of a most durable kind.

NOTES

An earlier version of this paper was read at the annual meeting of the American Anthropological Association, Cincinnati, December 1979.

1. Personal religious narratives of the type described herein are not restricted to the black branch of the Primitive Baptist church. I have collected similar narratives from white Primitive Baptists in the same region, and while they take slightly different forms, they share a number of features with the black examples.

2. I have edited these narrative excerpts for smoothness, eliminating pauses and errors.

REFERENCES

Boles, John B., 1972. *The Great Revival: 1787–1805* (Lexington: University of Kentucky Press).
Eliade, Mircea, 1963. *Myth and Reality* (New York: Harper and Row).
Finney, Charles G., 1973. *Memoirs of Rev. Charles G. Finney, Written by Himself* (New York: AMS Press).
Frye, Northrop, 1957. *Anatomy of Criticism: Four Essays* (Princeton: Princeton University Press).
Johnson, Clifton H., ed., 1969. *God Struck Me Dead: Religious Conversion Experiences and Autobiographies of Ex-Slaves* (Philadelphia: Pilgrim Press).
Lévy-Bruhl, Lucien, 1926 (trans. Lilian A. Clare). *How Natives Think* (London: George Allen and Unwin).
Moody, William R., 1931. *D. L. Moody* (New York: Macmillan).
Ricoeur, Paul, 1966 (trans. Erazim V. Kohak). *Freedom and Nature: The Voluntary and the Involuntary* (Evanston: Northwestern University Press).

Shea, Daniel B., 1968. *The Spiritual Autobiography in Early America* (Princeton: Princeton University Press).

Spacks, Patricia Meyer, 1976. *Imagining a Self: Autobiography and Novel in Eighteenth-Century England* (Cambridge: Harvard University Press).

Turner, Victor, 1969. *The Ritual Process: Structure and Anti-Structure* (Chicago: Aldine).

Van Gennep, Arnold, 1960. *The Rites of Passage* (London: Routledge and Kegan Paul).

Wesley, John, 1938. *The Journal of the Rev. John Wesley*, vol. 1, Nehemiah Curnock, ed. (London: Epworth Press).

Comments on Part Two

JAMES L. PEACOCK

The vast literature on the American South tends to fall into several major categories, each subdivided by discipline or approach. One category comprises studies of the southern "great tradition." These studies expound central themes, values, and institutions of the regional mainstream, or "high," culture. Examples are W. J. Cash's *The Mind of the South*, from journalism; Clement Eaton's *The Growth of Southern Civilization*, from history; Samuel S. Hill's *Southern Churches in Crisis*, from religion; C. Hugh Holman's *Three Modes of Southern Fiction*, from literature; V. O. Key's *Southern Politics in State and Nation*, from political science; and John Reed's *The Enduring South*, from sociology. Considering that the subjects covered by these works range from such raw types as Faulkner's Snopses to populist politicians like Huey Long and Gene Talmadge, the term "high" may seem unsuitable; what is meant is the dominant, or mainstream, culture.

A second group treats folk, or "little," traditions. Those by folklorists have been mainly collections and studies of specific genres of folklore—Cecil Sharp's *English Folksongs from the Southern Appalachians*, or Bruce Jackson's *Wake Up Dead Men: Afro-American Worksongs from Texas Prisons*. One could also include here historical interpretation of narratives from slaves, mountaineers, or yeoman farmers.

A third group, which includes anthropological studies, focuses on the community or other aspects of social organization. Here would fit the studies surveyed by John K. Morland in *The Not So Solid South* as well as later works, such as Carol Stack's *All Our Kin* and most of the essays presented in the first part of this volume.

Useful and provocative as such studies are, one crucial stream has yet to be adequately incorporated into the scholarly vision of the South. This stream of culture is outside the Great Tradition, and it has many traits of the little, or folk, cultures. Yet it is literate. Grounded in community life to an extent, it transcends localized roots and settings, and hence is not adequately comprehended by the community-study or social-organization framework. I refer to the sectarian groups—the Pentecostals, the German Brethren, the Primitive Baptists, and many others, of varying ethnic background, whether black, white, red, or even Asian.

In some ways, these groups are not properly termed southern, although they are located in the South (as well as elsewhere), and in some instances originated in the South. German Baptists of Virginia, for example, look toward kindred groups in the Midwest, Pennsylvania, or Canada. Primitive Baptists in the North Carolina mountains travel freely up the valleys to Pennsylvania or down to Alabama, but seem to perceive the Piedmont section of their state as a distant place. Pentecostals in Durham describe Dunn, in eastern North Carolina, as a historic center of their sect—along with Los Angeles, California. We need to keep in mind the complex relations, perceptual as well as geographic, between these sectarian groups and the southern regional identity.

A methodological dimension also should be noted. Southern studies to date have not fully elaborated the relations between that which is central to these sects—their living, vital, spiritual life embodied in ritual forms—and the social and cultural contexts as well as the historical roots of these forms. Folklorists have traditionally treated forms rather in isolation. Anthropologists have laid out the social and cultural contexts without sufficiently focusing on the forms themselves. And historians of southern religion are forced by their subject to rely on past accounts—or, in the case of oral historians, accounts of the past—rather than enjoying the direct observation and experience of living ritual that is possible through fieldwork. If the papers here ignore the community context and the historical background of the forms they describe, this is in part a deliberate effort to correct a balance—to focus especially on the ritual experience and the expressive forms that have been neglected in previous studies. Certainly the authors do not deny the sociological and historical dimensions; indeed, most of them treat these aspects in other places. As the African proverb has it, to say that one has a father is not to deny that one has a mother.

The papers vary in approach and thematic emphasis. Sutton focuses on the narrative of grace, especially the account of visions, a pattern that he reveals by a subtle portrayal which itself carries narrative power. Forrest addresses a theoretical question by an ethnographic case and argues that only certain aesthetic forms suit the process of provoking conversion. Williams also treats the conversion experience, but more ethnographically, and Grindal evokes the general world of the black religious life especially in relation to the notion of God and Devil. Despite their variety, together the papers comprise a cluster of themes generally taken as central in the southern religious experience: the dramatic conversion experience and its narration, healing, preaching, humor, and the threat of the Devil.

What should be stressed about these papers is that they are accounts from anthropologists just returned from fieldwork, or even still in the midst of it. While interpretation is given, the emphasis is on the presentation of fresh ethnographic data. These kinds of accounts will be invaluable for future syntheses. Consider what dimensions might have been added to such a seminal work as Donald Matthew's *Religion in the Old South* if anthropologists with their tape recorders had been in the antebellum churches.

Ethnically, both blacks and whites are portrayed. Absent are such Native American churches as those of the Lumbe and Cherokee, Choctaw and Seminole.

In short, these papers constitute an extremely valuable evocation of what a William James might term "Varieties of Southern Religious Experience" — slices of life soundly based in fieldwork, reported with freshness and immediacy.

Part Three

Land Tenure and Social Policies

Peasants and Policy:
Comparative Perspectives on Aging

B. Lisa Gröger

This essay has two parts and one theme. The first part is based on data collected in a different South, the southern half of France, where I did fieldwork from June 1975 to December 1976. The second part is based on certain assumptions I have made on the basis of my research in France. Some of these assumptions I mean to explore in the South of the United States. The theme is how certain policy measures affect the lives of individuals, and how policy creates certain resources which people manipulate and which manipulate people. Following a brief summary of the salient features of French agriculture, I shall discuss one particular policy measure, its stated objectives, its alleged effect on a national scale, and finally its actual consequences in a community of small farmers. Then I shall outline my recently begun study among small tobacco farmers in the Piedmont region of North Carolina, where I am exploring the effects of the politics of tobacco on the lives of the rural elderly.

The two most striking features of French agriculture today are its relatively large labor force and the persistence of small farms side by side with large capitalistic farms. The big farms are concentrated in the flat and fertile North and produce monocrops on a large scale. Small family farms prevail in the West, the Southwest, and the Massif Central, where the terrain is hilly, the land poor, and the returns from agriculture low (Dovring 1956:153; Franklin 1969:77–78).

The municipality of Landous, where this research was conducted, belongs to the family-farming region of France. It is located in Aveyron, a *département* in the southern foothills of the Massif Central. Unlike many other disadvantaged areas, this part of Aveyron still has young people who are willing to stay in agriculture. They are said to be enthusiastic about machinery and to have "absolute confidence in technical progress" (Fél 1962:308). However, if one talks with the farmers, their enthusiasm is not always apparent. Farmers in Landous expressed great concern about mechanization. They used the term synonymously with "progress," and its meaning was ambiguous if not outright negative.

Their mixed agriculture with its emphasis on animal-raising requires many machines on small farms. The average size of holding is 60 acres. Farmers in Landous produce for the market six-month-old calves, cow's milk, sheep, piglets, fattened pigs, and barnyard produce. All animals except fattened pigs are raised on crops grown on the farm. Many farmers hybridize seed corn under contract. All grow feed corn; most grow some wheat, barley, and rye, and a few grow tobacco. All produce a large part of their own food. In the many discussions about progress, farmers in Landous, big and small alike, unanimously claimed that machines were ruining them. How then do they manage to continue their farming operation from one year to the next, and from one generation to the next?

French family farms were the object of extensive legislation in 1960 and 1962. The choice of policy consisted basically of two alternatives: to subsidize family farms, or not to subsidize them, thus allowing large-scale capitalist farms to take over the total agricultural production, presumably without state aid. The French government opted for the first alternative. It promised to favor and promote the type of family farm which was "susceptible to making optimal use of modern production techniques and to utilize fully its labor and capital" (Code Rural 1976:456–57). The definition of the family farm was based on two units of labor, with "a man working on the farm 300 days per year, 9 hours per day" counted as one unit of labor (Lefebvre 1976:1003).

One of the major objectives of the legislation was to consolidate the multitude of small and fragmented holdings into bigger ones that would be better able to mechanize efficiently. This restructuring of landholdings was to be achieved through certain social measures. Specifically, land was to be consolidated by the gradual removal from agriculture of the older farmers. Their land would then be absorbed by neighboring holdings, making these holdings more viable. Annual pre-retirement and retirement premiums are granted for life to old farmers if they sell or rent their land, or if they relinquish farm management. The annual amount of the pre-retirement premium in 1975 was $960 for an unmarried, widowed, or divorced person, and $1,440 for a couple or for a single person with one or more dependent children. As a supplement to old-age pension, the premium was $300 for everybody. After her husband's death, a woman receives two-thirds of his premium.

Bureaucrats consider the premium scheme the generator of structural change. The scheme is said to release 2.4 million acres annually (OECD 1972:136). By 1971, it had allegedly released 20 percent of all of the farmland in the country (OECD 1974:62). The figures for Aveyron are no less impressive. According to the General Agricultural Census of 1970, the premiums had a great impact in the *département*. They were said to have helped "to accelerate a certain restructuring." By the end of 1974, 10,500 farmers, or half of all the farms in Aveyron, were receiving the premium (DDA 1974). Yet the rhetoric about the success of the premiums, supported by impressive statistics, does not always depict accurately what happens. A closer look at the role of the premiums in Landous will reveal a part of reality which is masked by the statistics. I shall argue that the granting of the premium has not led to a significant restructuring of farms. It *has* speeded up the succession of young farm operators who, being young, were eligible for long-term credit and who were willing to make large investments. After the young operators took over, there was a dramatic increase in the indebtedness of farms.

In 1976, 80 of the 114 farmers in Landous were receiving the premium. The total amount of land "released" was 4,322 acres, or 56 percent of the farmland of the municipality. However, of these 80 cases, only 23 had resulted in some restructuring of holdings. That is, the land of 23 holdings was absorbed by other holdings. These 23 holdings had been small. Their smallness had predisposed them to being absorbed by others: the heirs to these holdings could not have made a living from farming such small units, and they had therefore left agriculture. Because of their smallness, these holdings did not contribute to a significant restructuring. Their average size was 31 acres. The amount of land transferred by their dissolution was 719 acres. The other 57 premiums were granted for the transmission of the management of holdings to a son, a son-in-law, or a daughter.

In 1976, the average annual retirement premium in Landous of $400 was hardly a strong incentive for giving up one's land. But why not take it anyway since, in the case of a son's succeeding his father, it costs nothing? The only risk associated with the premium, loss of control over one's land, is irrelevant in cases of succession by the person who would have succeeded anyway. In these cases, the result of the "certain restructuring" attributed to the premium is not a larger farm. Rather, the result is a new type of operator who is more likely to accept progress.

Between 1965 and 1971, agricultural debts in Aveyron increased by 230 percent; the number of farm loans went up 251 percent (Ministry of Agriculture 1972:82). During the same period, most of the premiums were granted. It is reasonable to assume that this dramatic increase in agricultural loans is related to the changing age of farm operators. My data from Landous support the assumption that there was an increase in investment during the years immediately following the premium-related succession.

Farms which received the premium had a higher mean annual investment than those which did not receive the premium. They also had a considerably greater increase in investment during the five years following the premium-related succession than their non-premium-receiving counterparts during a comparable period. This increase was 127 percent on farms not receiving the premium, and 423 percent on farms receiving the premium. During the five-year period preceding the granting of the premium, those farms that later did receive the premium had been lagging behind the others in investment. This reflects the reluctance of old men to invest. Once succession had taken place, investment surpassed that of farmers not receiving the premium both in relative and absolute terms.[1]

The effect of the retirement premium in a community of farmers is very different from that stated by the policymakers who support their claims with misleading statistics. Comparable statistics for Landous would have us believe that the premiums have "liberated" 56 percent of the farmland of the municipality. Actually, the land which was transferred as a result of the premium and which led to the minimal enlargement of neighboring holdings, represented less than ten percent of the farmland of Landous. In an area of small farms, this can hardly be considered a significant improvement of the agrarian structure. The most significant effect of the premium was a dramatic increase in investment and indebtedness following the official but not necessarily actual transmission of farm management from father to son, son-in-law, or daughter.

What are the implications of this result? I think that the most important one is the young farmer's commitment of his labor to the farm. Keeping young farmers from leaving is a remarkable feat in this area of stem-family organization where the prospective heir's leaving is a constant threat for several reasons. The living together of three generations offers limited privacy and autonomy to the prospective heir. Fathers do not easily relinquish management. Here the situation is not as extreme as in Ireland, where succession and marriage are closely linked, resulting in late marriage (Arensberg and Kimball 1968). In France, presuccession marriage may relieve sexual tensions, but it creates others, specifically tensions between women who are outsiders, and conflicts of authority between father and son. Traditionally, a son may have had different ideas from his father's, but he had no authority to implement them. Now, under the retirement premium scheme, officially the son does have the authority, granted to him through state intervention. It would be naive, however, to believe that this legislation eradicated overnight the old authority pattern. Three generations continue to live together. The father continues to work on the farm. He may disagree with his son's management decisions. While he cannot stop him from implementing these decisions, he can make his life miserable. Instead of testing the limits of authority, most parties make compromises. Thus, in many cases, the transmission of farm management from father to son takes place on paper only. The tensions that have characterized this type of productive and reproductive organization continue to exist. In addition, the son is now tied to the farm through debts. He has committed his labor to farming under conditions of hard work and low returns on his investments, no return on his labor, and to financing mechanization through his labor.

How does the monetary aspect of the premiums affect older persons and their status vis-à-vis other members of the household? As we have seen, the premium is relatively small. However, the effect of the policy becomes clearer if one also considers old-age pensions. Two-thirds of the farmers in Landous received old-age pensions averaging $2,200 annually. These payments are a crucial supplement to farm income, especially for the smaller holdings. In many cases, these payments approach the equivalent of farm income. While all social categories in France receive old-age pensions, the effect of these payments is different among the agricultural population. Equivalent amounts go a longer way in the rural setting, where most of the food consumed by the family is produced on the farm. Much of the pension and retirement premium payments is plowed back into farm production. People often stated that without these payments they would not have been able to buy certain farm machines. Old people who receive the premium and/or a pension may buy a farm machine for the family farm. They give presents of clothes and other items—such as transistor radios, bicycles, and school supplies—to their grandchildren. They also give them cash, and they make important contributions to their trousseaux. By doing so, they liberate equivalent amounts from the family-farm budget for use on the farm. Giving to their children and grandchildren represents the major area of expenditure for retired farmers. Few of the old men, and none of the old women, drive cars. They may buy a new garment once in a while. Men may spend some money on tobacco, and all of them probably spend some money on alcohol, but most of their resources are made available to the household in one of the manners mentioned above—unless the money is put into savings, in which case it will be spent by the household later on.

When talking about agricultural production and the difficulty of working the land, several young people stated jokingly that in this area, the major crop was old people, and that this crop had to be tended lovingly. The control of cash from a source off the farm has given the old people a means for rewarding those on whom they have, or will, become physically dependent. If they had to live off their pensions in another environment, they might be destitute. Living as they do, their retirement payments constitute an important resource that most of them manipulate successfully: they transform it into tender loving care. The fact that this care may in some cases be given ambivalently matters little for this analysis. What matters is that the kin group, with all its asymmetrical rights and obligations, and with its inherent conflicts and tensions, becomes a major resource (Stack 1974:73–78).

Let us now look at rural aging in North Carolina, in a community I shall call Mayfield and a county I shall call Piedmont. My guiding assumption in this research is that the politics of tobacco influence greatly the conditions and status of aging farmers, and shape the relationship between persons of different generations. The key resource here is a product of government policy, tobacco allotments, or the permission to grow and market tobacco.

Through the Agricultural Adjustment Act of 1933, tobacco allotments were granted to farms with a history of growing tobacco. Because tobacco production was not mechanized then and labor was a limiting factor, the original allotments were small, ranging from three to five acres per farm. With the advent of mechanization and its concomitant logic of ever-larger farms, allotments have become a scarce resource. While the demand for allotments has increased, no new allotments are being granted. The rationale for adopting the allotment system was to guarantee a livelihood to small farmers and thus prevent nonfarmers from buying up farmland as an investment, and to control the supply of tobacco. Until 1965, only the acreage was limited. Then a limit on marketable pounds was added to stop farmers from overfertilizing their allotted acreage and thus from producing a huge crop of low quality.[2]

Stringent rules and regulations surround every aspect of tobacco production. If an allotment is idle for more than five years, it will be taken away from the farm and put back into the reserve of the county. In Piedmont County, the reserve of tobacco allotments available for 1980 was 1.84 acres. Obviously, this does not allow for a significant expansion of production on any given farm, especially since the 1.84 acres of allotment are to be equitably distributed among those who need it most.

Although new allotments can be granted only to qualified growers, many of the older allotments now belong to nonfarmers, mainly as a result of estate divisions, but also as a result of farm sales. In the settlement of estates, allotments are divided down to a hundredth of an acre to make shares equal, and often heirs will fight over a hundredth. If cropland that has a tobacco allotment on it is sold, the corresponding proportion of the allotment has to be sold with the land unless the buyer renounces it in a written agreement.

Tobacco allotments affect the price of land significantly. In Piedmont County, any tobacco allotment sold with land adds between two to three dollars per pound to the price of land. Thus, three acres of land with one acre, or 1,500 pounds, of tobacco allotment, will cost between $3,000 to $4,000 *more* than the same land without the allotment.

An aging farmer who cannot or does not want to farm any longer has a number of options. He can take a tenant who pays either a cash rent or a share of the crop. He can sell his land with his allotment, or he can keep some or all of his land and lease the tobacco allotment to another farmer who would like to grow more than his own allotment. Such leases are made on a yearly basis and are permissible only within counties.

The price for leasing tobacco allotments has increased much more than the price paid for tobacco. In 1975, a pound leased for 5 cents and sold for $1.00;

in 1979, a pound of tobacco allotment leased for 35 or 40 cents, and a pound of tobacco sold for $1.35. A number of good years had led many farmers to mechanize and to produce more tobacco. More tobacco required more curing barns. To justify the investment, such a farmer had to continue to produce more tobacco—that is, continue to lease tobacco allotments—no matter what the cost. The demand for leasing drove up the price. Someone who owned five acres of tobacco allotment (the average size of allotments in Mayfield) in 1979 could net $3,150 (or half of the median family income for the county) simply by signing a lease. Clearly, the high leasing price works to the advantage of old persons who own tobacco allotments.

An inventory of farms in Mayfield revealed several categories of farms: farms without tobacco allotments; farms that lease their tobacco allotment to others; farms that grow their own tobacco allotment; farms that grow their own and others' tobacco allotment; and farms not worked by their owner. The inventory also revealed these categories of individuals: those who own but do not work land; those who work but do not own land; and those who work and own land. These categories reflect the life cycle of rural families and the class structure of this agrarian-based community, and are relevant to a study of rural aging. Although only approximately 40 families in the community are *farmers*, many more individuals, if not all members of the community, are tied together through *farming*. Many retired farmers own land and tobacco allotments. Tobacco allotments constitute the major productive resource in a community totally dependent on this crop. Allotment leases are a subsistence base for many elderly persons; they are also the basis for many social relationships throughout the community. I am assuming that the quality of life of elderly allotment-owners depends on how they manage this resource. Control or lack of control of this resource ties all categories of individuals together in interdependence. The ability of a relatively few (40) full-time farmers to stay in business depends on the willingness of many (235) allotment owners to continue the leasing arrangements, which in turn represent an important source of income for them. Finally, the working of the system rests on the labor of those who do not own land: ascending sons, lifelong tenants, and the many day laborers and migrant laborers who do not enter into the statistics.

In the course of this research, I expect to find not only differences in the ownership of tobacco allotments but also differences in the skills with which older persons manipulate this scarce resource to their advantage. The questions I am exploring include the following: When and under what circumstances do farmers retire? How do variations in land tenure, farm size, and inheritance practices affect the conditions and status of aging farmers? How does race affect access to land and to tobacco allotments? (The majority of landowners are white, while the majority of tenants are black.) Are leasing arrangements stable over time? What is the motivation (for example, residential proximity, kinship, friendship, debts) for leasing to, or leasing from, a particular individual? What is the nature of personal involvements between lessor and lessee?

The politics of tobacco seem to have safeguarded the small family farm by dispersing the major productive resource among many owners, and by making producers dependent upon a single crop. Whether and to what extent the politics of tobacco have kept nonfarmers from buying up farmland will emerge from my statistical survey of land transactions for the county over the last ten years. Of the 410 farm divisions, 90 percent fell into four major categories: (1) partial farm sale including part of the tobacco allotment; (2) partial farm sale with the parent farm retaining the total tobacco allotment; (3) division of the land and the tobacco allotment among multiple heirs; and (4) total farm sale. Categories 2 and 3 appear to channel land into the hands of nonfarmers, though not necessarily out of farming, for such land often continues to be worked by a farmer.

Finally I shall compare the effect of policy in France with that in North Carolina. My research in France has shown a discrepancy between the official intent of policy and its actual effect. It raises the question whether the survival of the small family farm is desirable at any cost—especially if the cost is carried by the farm family in question. The particular French policy measure discussed above is only one of a series. Elsewhere (Gröger 1979) I have shown that, taken together, the various policy measures make up a policy that encourages minimally viable farms to increase their production, to mechanize heavily, and to go heavily into debt. The policy leads small farmers to compete fiercely with each other for land that is extremely scarce. Since most farmers cannot enlarge their farms, they intensify their fodder production to keep more animals. More animals require more investment and more labor. Subsequent recourse to labor-saving machines invariably results not only in more capital outlay but also in more work. Only by exploiting their family labor can these small farmers finance their investment. By intensifying their labor, they have helped to make France a major exporter of food. By intensifying their capital investment, they have become important consumers of machines. Given this situation, one is led to wonder how intentional the allegedly unintended consequences of policy are.

One parallel between the French agricultural policy and the politics of tobacco in the United States is that both governments have committed themselves to safeguarding the small family farm. Why would the US government want small tobacco farms? Even if at its origin the tobacco allotment system was well-intentioned—that is, to protect small farmers from the Depression—the original intention does not necessarily explain why the system still functions. I think we have to look beyond the government for an answer.[3] The tobacco lobby in the United States is powerful. By inducing the government to keep farms small through price supports coupled with a tight control on production, the tobacco companies assure themselves of a reliable supply of tobacco without taking on the risk of production themselves. Big farms would be much less dependent on tobacco. They could produce other things, such as grains or meat, which do not require government permission but do require more land to make a living. As it is, most farms in the Piedmont region are too small to produce grains or meat. Having become dependent on tobacco, the farmers themselves have a stake in, and are proponents of, the continuation of the tobacco program.

Nevertheless, the politics of tobacco has entered a new phase. The antismoking campaigns have led to a drop in US tobacco consumption. Also, the contradiction between a government-sponsored antismoking campaign on the one hand, and government subsidy of tobacco production on the other, is becoming increasingly absurd. While the tobacco companies are trying to expand their exports, a number of individuals and groups have begun to talk about alternative crops. Truck farming would be one alternative to tobacco, but at the present time there are no marketing structures for such produce even though there may be a demand. I met a farmer who had tried to liberate himself from the constraints of tobacco. He built two greenhouses and had no difficulty growing tomatoes. He did have difficulty selling them. No supermarket was interested in the small quantities he had to offer. There were no growers' cooperatives, and he found that he could either tend his crop or sell it at the farmers' market, but that he could not do both. He went back to planting tobacco.

Given the small scale of tobacco production in this area, and the intermittent labor requirement, many tobacco farmers also work off the farm. Possibly the marginal security of their farm allows them to work for low wages in off-farm employment. Data to be collected on household income composition from all persons contributing to it will reveal whether off-farm wages are partly used to finance the farming operation. If so, such a finding would dispel the notion that industrial employment invariably leads people to abandon farming. In this case, industrial employment may well make it possible for small farmers to stay in business. Such farmers who use their off-farm wages for their agricultural production would be very different from large capitalistic farmers who must make a profit. Who says there are no peasants in the United States?

NOTES

Funds for my fieldwork in France were provided by the National Science Foundation (Grant Number SOC75-13099), the Social Science Research Council (Dissertation

Fellowship and Write-up Award), the National Institute of Mental Health (Training Grant 5-TO-MH-12493), and Columbia University, all of whom I wish to thank for their support. I am grateful to the Center for the Study of Aging and Human Development, Duke University, for partial support from grant 5 T32 AG00029 from the National Institute on Aging. I also wish to thank Carol Stack for letting me present an earlier version of this paper to her postdoctoral fellows at the Institute of Policy Sciences at Duke University, who made helpful suggestions.

1. The discussion of investment is based on data from machine inventories of 34 farms in Alunhac, a rural parish and an administrative section of the municipality of Landous. Of the 20 retirement premiums granted in Alunhac, 15 were granted between 1965 and 1970. For details, see Gröger 1979:116–26.

2. For a concise history of the tobacco program and the economics of tobacco production, see Mann 1975.

3. As Mann 1975:33–50 points out, there is no such thing as *the* government. Rather, there are a multitude of interest groups with different or conflicting objectives. These groups include the tobacco growers, themselves divided and belonging to organizations whose objectives differ; the warehousemen; the tobacco companies; hired labor; sharecroppers; the land-grant colleges; local tradesmen and bankers; the smokers; and the antismoking forces. All of them have at one time or another sought to influence members of the Senate and House Agriculture Committees on decisions concerning tobacco.

REFERENCES

Arensberg, Conrad M., and Solon Kimball, 1968. *Family and Community in Ireland*, 2nd ed. (Cambridge: Harvard University Press).

Code Rural, 1976. (Paris: Jurisprudence Générale Dalloz).

DDA, 1974. *Statistiques Agricoles* (Rodez: Direction Départementale de l'Agriculture).

Dovring, Folke, 1956. *Land and Labor in Europe, 1900–1950* (The Hague: Martinus Nijhoff).

Fél, André, 1962. *Les Hautes Terres du Massif Central: Tradition Paysanne et Economie Agricole*, Faculté des Lettres et Sciences Humaines de Clermont-Ferrant.

Franklin, S. H., 1969. *The European Peasantry: The Final Phase* (London: Methuen).

Gröger, B. Lisa, 1979. *The Transformation of Peasants into Consumers of Machines: Big Tractors on Small Fields in a French Community* (Ph.D. diss., Columbia University).

Lefebvre, Francis, 1976. *Mémento Pratique de l'Agriculture* (Paris: Edition Francis Lefebvre).

Mann, Charles Kellogg, 1975. *Tobacco: The Ants and the Elephants* (Salt Lake City: Olympus).

Ministry of Agriculture, 1972. *Aveyron 1972: Etude Départementale d'Aménagement Rural* (Paris: Imprimerie Nationale).

OECD, 1972. *Structural Reform Measures in Agriculture* (Paris: Organization for Economic Cooperation and Development).

———, 1974. *Agricultural Policy in France* (Paris: Organization for Economic Cooperation and Development).

Stack, Carol B., 1974. *All Our Kin: Strategies for Survival in a Black Community* (New York: Harper and Row).

The Last of the Tenant Farmers in the Old New South: A Case Study of Tenancy in Franklin County, North Carolina

STEVEN PETROW

DOWN ON THE FARM: THE BLACK TENANT

In many respects, the rural South continues to be the white man's South. Despite more than a hundred years of emancipation, rural blacks remain tied to the land—most of them by a system of agricultural tenancy. Whereas tenancy remains a collecting ground for poor blacks, it has become a system of upward mobility for lower- and middle-class whites. Most of the economic and social opportunities attached to tenancy are allocated exclusively to white tenants, who, for the most part, belong to the cash-tenant class. In contrast, sharecroppers, most of whom are black, continue to disappear from government reports commensurate to the rate with which they are displaced by external forces and with which they fail at the marketplace. Despite some progress, my contention is that the South is geared to white mobility and based on the perpetuation of black stability.

The depth of poverty for black farm families is striking on a quantitative level, one reflecting the enormous difference in median family income based on race. For blacks, the median farm family income is $4,857; the amount for whites is nearly three times that figure—$11,237 (US Bureau of the Census 1977). In 1976, 43.2 percent of the black farm population earned less than $4,000, while only 13.5 percent of the white farm population fell within these limits.

However, the qualitative differences in black/white conditions appear to be even more severe. Nowhere are the doubts about changes in the New South more valid or visible than in the class and race differences distinguished by the three basic types of tenant farming: cash-tenancy, cash-share farming, and sharecropping. Historically, race has been a powerful agent of economic differentiation in the South, but to consider the race issue apart from class distinction is to deny certain human relationships and societal forces that continue to exploit and to bankrupt the lowest ranks. Gunnar Myrdal described the various levels of tenancy in 1944, a pattern that still holds true today: "There are great differences in economic status and degree of dependency between the several types of tenants. Highest on the ladder are the renters and the cash-tenants, who rent their farms for a fixed sum of money. Cash-tenants can usually be regarded as independent entrepreneurs. . . . All other kinds of arrangements entitle the landlord to a certain share of the main cash crop . . . sometimes even as much as three-fourths. Those lowest down have little or nothing but their labor to offer" (Myrdal 1944:236).

Racial differences are implied in the disproportion of blacks in the lower socioeconomic strata. Of all black tenants, 92 percent are categorized as sharecroppers, the lowest rank; 84 percent of white tenants are croppers. Conversely, the percentage of white tenants who are cash-renters is twice the percentage of black tenants who farm that way; the value of the average white cash-tenant's farm is four times that of the average black cash-tenant's farm (US Bureau of the Census 1964).[1] These figures and others indicate that nearly 45 percent of all black tenants work farms valued at less than $10,000. Other statistics, such as those in Table 1, clearly point out the disparity between whites and blacks within each tenure group.

Incomes of tenants in Franklin County, North Carolina, show the same disparities by class and within class by race, except in the sharecropper class, where no income differential was found (see Table 2). But of the five sharecroppers I interviewed about income, four were black. Empirical data derived from these interviews clearly establish the economic advantages of

Table 1. Median Incomes for Black and White Tenant Farmers, North Carolina, 1964

	LESS THAN $5,000	MORE THAN $5,000	% EARNING $5,000+
	Blacks		
Cash-tenants	$1,275	—	0%
Cash-share tenants	1,058	$16,280*	1.6
Sharecroppers	874	7,218	3.4
	Whites		
Cash-tenants	$1,734	$8,280	15.6%
Cash-share tenants	1,529	7,940	10.6
Sharecroppers	1,193	8,271	6.7

SOURCE: US Bureau of the Census 1964:73 (Table 18a).

*This figure is clearly an anomaly, as it is derived from the income of only four wage-earners.

Table 2. Median Incomes for Black and White Tenant Farmers in Franklin County, North Carolina, 1978

	Blacks	*Whites*
Cash-tenants	$9,000	$22,000
Cash-share tenants	3,250	46,000*
Sharecroppers	1,000	1,000*

*Figure is derived from one household.

cash-tenancy over subordinate arrangements, including cash-sharing and sharecropping.

A cash-tenant is an independent operator pending payment of his rent. Usually, he arranges his own loans. Often, he owns both his farm equipment and his house. Cash-share tenancy, on the other hand, combines aspects of both renting and crop-sharing. The usual arrangement requires the cash-share tenant to own some of his equipment—tractors or trucks—but not necessarily barns and more sophisticated equipment. The cash-share tenant pays a flat rental fee, the same as the cash-tenant, plus a share of the crop yield. Expenses are apportioned according to the amount of equipment the cash-share tenant provides. The cash-share tenant, like the renter, arranges his own credit. Since many tenant farmers do not own land, securing loan guarantees is often difficult. Three cash-share tenants targeted by this study, all of whom were black, did not begin a renting arrangement until the mid-1960s, when their grown children, living in the North, were able to send home regular checks.

Obviously, there is a high positive correlation between farm income and the number of acres under cultivation. In tenured farm holdings, the average acreage of black tenants was about half that of white tenants. Furthermore, statistics indicate that while 41 percent of the tenant farmer population is black, blacks farm only 26 percent of the available land (US Bureau of the Census 1964). Historically, whites have farmed, on the average, greater numbers of acres than blacks. Moreover, it should be noted that the average cash-tenant's farm is worth three times that of the sharecropper—usually because of the greater number of acres farmed.

Exactly why a sharecropper's yield on an acre will bring less than a cash-share or renter arrangement can be explained in the following way. Normally, an acre of tobacco will yield between 1,600 and 2,000 pounds of tobacco, depending on the quality of the land. Each acre has a yield figure computed by the United States Department of Agriculture based on previous harvests. In 1977, tobacco sold for about $1.07 a pound in Franklin County. Thus, there was a $428 difference between the lowest and highest yields per acre that year. The cash-tenant and the cash-share tenant paid approximately 35 cents a pound of tobacco as rent to the landlord. These tenants then had a profit of between 72 and 77 cents per pound. Based on a median figure of 22 acres per cash-tenant, gross profit would have been about $31,000 before expenses. Less fuel and production costs, the cash-tenant should have realized a net income of about $17,800.[2]

The median number of acres farmed by the sharecropper, however, is closer to four. His gross profit would have totaled between $6,988 and $8,560, again depending upon yield. After production costs, his profit would have ranged between $4,588 and $6,160. After settling with his landlord, the sharecropper should have received half of the net earnings—in this case, between $2,300 and $3,080. Often, however, he does not get this amount because the landlord will subtract all loans plus interest that the cropper may have accrued during the year. It is not unusual for a sharecropper to borrow $100 a month between March and September. Discounting interest payments, his indebtedness prior to the harvest averages between $600 and $700. The sharecropper is left with an adjusted net income of between $1,600 and $2,400 for an entire year's work. The landlord, however, would receive from $750 to $950 per tobacco acre, or an average of $3,000 to $3,800 per cropper. In other words, the landlord will earn twice what each of his sharecroppers makes.

The renter and the cash-share tenant, in addition to their principal cash crop, maintain other sources of income, usually by farming several other crops. Sharecroppers generally do not.

From 1950 to 1964, when the full effects of mechanization were first being realized, tenants from all classes and races were displaced in great numbers. As might be expected, the lowest economic groups, and especially blacks, suffered the greatest losses (see Table 3).

Cash-tenants, who own their homes, tended not to move, and many sharecroppers have not moved either. One woman, the widow of a black sharecropper, still resides in the same house with her four children where, in 1923, she was born. She farms with the son of the man with whom her father contracted in the 1930s and 1940s. Her 72-year-old mother lives just down the road. Another sharecropper, a white man, has worked for the same farmer since 1945. He and his wife retired in 1975 and continue to live in the house owned by the landlord. The annual incomes of both families are well under $2,000 each.

A great many whites consider black mobility "an act of aggression"; consequently, in the past landlords took steps to prevent a tenant from leaving, sometimes threatening to "clean 'im up—to take his hogs, his corn, and all his possessions" (Powdermaker 1939:80). Yet the sharecropper, threatened with displacement, was more likely to relocate, though transition was often difficult for him. Many croppers followed patterns of regular relocation, changing landlords as often as every two years. Such families were optimistic

Table 3. Average Acreages Worked by Tenant Farmers in North Carolina

	1930	*1950*	*1964*
All tenants	48.8	47.4	59.4
All black tenants	42.0	39.7	37.7
All white tenants	53.7	53.4	74.7
All cash-tenants	62.9	64.2	64.5
Black cash-tenants	54.2	53.5	44.2
White cash-tenants	66.2	68.6	70.3
All cash-sharers	n.a.	58.4	86.2
Black cash-sharers	n.a.	47.4	57.8
White cash-sharers	n.a.	66.1	92.4
All sharecroppers	n.a.	45.1	55.3
Black sharecroppers	n.a.	38.9	37.2
White sharecroppers	n.a.	50.8	69.8

SOURCE: US Bureau of the Census 1964:10.
n.a.: not available.

and zealous in their pursuit of better tobacco allotments, furnishings, and other tangibles. They uniformly believed that they could improve their situation. They also wanted the satisfaction of knowing that they had tried to change their circumstances, that they had not let themselves become "tied to the land." Nearly all of these sharecroppers worked for at least eight landlords during their lifetimes.

Ironically, these less sedentary farmers earned no more, farmed no greater tracts, and lived in houses of no better quality than those sharecroppers seemingly resigned to their situation. It is not surprising that feelings of disinheritance and disillusionment have in turn had a great impact on the general disenfranchisement of the cropping class. None of the sharecroppers, black or white, has ever run for any elective office or served on an appointed county commission. Nor do they attend town council and school board meetings.

TENANT FARMING: CROP VERSUS CASH

Since the mid-1930s, southern tenancy has been undergoing a systematic evolution. In that period, the ratio of white tenants to black tenants has increased steadily while the total population has declined. According to the Census Bureau, "Historically, higher rates of population loss among Black farm residents have been associated with heavy losses in the number of cotton and tobacco tenant farmers. Blacks have had a disproportionate representation among tenant farmers, and the number of such farms has fallen steadily and sharply since 1935" (US Bureau of the Census 1977). Despite the decrease in the general tenant population, of both blacks and whites, the South has experienced a proportional growth of cash-tenancy and cash-share farming.

The process of who or how one becomes a cash-renter or a cash-share tenant is unclear. Hortense Powdermaker discussed this in her 1939 study of race relations in the postbellum South: "In order to become a renter, a tenant must be necessarily on a higher economic level than a sharecropper. His position has obvious advantages. Once he has attained the status of cash-tenant, owning his tools and implements, selecting his own seed, free to buy where he will and above all free to sell his own crop, he may look hopefully toward independence" (Powdermaker 1939:90).

Until World War II, tenant farming was synonymous with severe poverty, despite the small number of more successful tenants. Following the war, large-scale renting became a more lucrative form of tenancy for many landowners, since the cash transaction was usually completed before the spring planting. This increased the immediate amount of capital the landowner had on hand to manage and finance his operation. However, this system of cash-renting was restricted to those tenants whose economic status enabled them to pay off large sums of money prior to harvest.

Because most tenants had few liquid assets, money was frequently borrowed. After the early 1940s, banking and other lending institutions became increasingly conservative in their fiscal policies. No longer was the crop considered sufficient collateral for a loan. Thus, new loans were almost always contingent upon landholdings. Banks and merchants introduced what was called a deed of trust, a lien on the land, which could be called to term at any time during the year it was due. If this happened, the tenant was left with two options: either he could settle his account or, more likely, he could forfeit his land in lieu of payment. Forfeitures were a common means by which land ownership shifted hands from a class of poor, small holders, both black and white, to a monied class of merchants and farmers, almost all of whom were white.

The increased use of cash in transactions between tenant and landlord has had far-reaching effects in the last four decades; perhaps most significant has been its part in the development of modern farming as a large, technological enterprise. However, it has also been integral in the destruction of the old, more economically relaxed system whereby family income was measured in terms of acres under cultivation or the number of hogs and livestock owned. Previously, barter had been an acceptable medium of transaction. With the onset of a cash-based economy, the trend in southern farming was away from those systems that were labor-intensive toward those that were capital-intensive. Consequently, the landowner, in order to finance his entry into the expanding world of mechanized farming, needed to secure cash in amounts much larger than before. With new machines and technology, most landlords and some tenants rapidly increased their landholdings and investments, working as much land as they could afford to buy or rent.

In this new cash economy, the essential distinction between types of tenure and, ultimately, between economic and social strata became one of ownership. Each stratum brings with it not only monetary advantages, but an increase in responsibility, self-management, and a general decline in the amount of economic and psychological dependence upon a landlord.

One particularly unfair aspect of the tenant system is that the amount of risk is most often shared equally between the landlord and the tenant, despite the fact that the tenant's actual investment is usually much less than the landlord's. Relative to the landlord, an enormous burden is placed on the tenant, while, in most other aspects of our economic community, it has been the accepted norm that the risk of investment should correspond directly with the size and importance of the investment. For most sharecroppers, a loss of just $1,000 or $2,000 can literally threaten their physical survival. A landowner, on the other hand, is better able to absorb losses, often into the thousands of dollars, sometimes by altering his life-style, but more frequently through programs underwritten by the state and designed to protect him in times of disaster through protracted repayment plans and low-interest loans.

CROPPIN': "A WAY TO KEEP FROM DYIN'"

In Franklin County, sharecroppers are unlike most other folks. As a group, they are black, with an occasional white who has not yet "raised his status." Many are older persons, but there are some younger families too, those without the means or the opportunities to find a better livelihood. There is a sense of vulnerability about them; most are thin, fragile, and many of the aged walk almost gingerly. The men have gray, thinned hair, deeply-set lines and wrinkles, discolored blotches on their faces. Some are hard of hearing, although none have "aids"; others are crippled by arthritis. During the winter months they wear thermal underwear, two pairs of socks, and heavy flannel shirts. The faded overalls and work boots are worn year round. Their wives tend to be large and heavy. Usually, the women will sit quietly during a discussion, mulling over each exchange; then, and without warning, they speak up. In their "free time," these women make their own dresses and do their own hair; they are always capable of looking out for themselves.

Some of them vote; others are afraid to register. Many prefer not to get involved. Nearly all of them are eligible for government assistance programs, but few apply. Certification is difficult. Most of them, however, do not want food stamps or any other "handout." "People don't like going up there for food stamps. I don't want to go up there. . . . They don't want you to have it. It's like it's their money."[3]

A sizeable portion of them cannot read. All that I talked with were permanently out of school by their tenth birthday.

> Mama took me out of school 'cause I had to help support the family. There was eight; I was the next-to-the-oldest boy. I went to school three or four years, but I didn't learn nothin'. I couldn't get my mind on my books. You go to school . . . and at 12 o'clock you got to go to work, and then in the morning you're right back in school. . . . You see it don't give you much time to think. It'll keep your mind all messed up.

Vance Reed, a black cropper, started working eight hours a day when he was ten years old. "You were always needed on the farm. You's come back from school and go to work. School was an hour away. You had to walk; when you got there you put your hands in a pot of hot water to numb 'em up."

Not being able to read meant that you could not understand the slip of paper the merchant gave you at the end of the year telling you how much you owed; it meant that you could not read about community meetings or agricultural-methods courses advertised in the newspapers; it meant that you were totally dependent on others to read documents, contracts, and all other written material. It meant that in one very important way you were helpless.

Although the schools were segregated, the black croppers grew up side-by-side with whites in the fields. Sometimes they were neighbors. One black sharecropper explained:

> I've been farmin' all my life ever since I was ten years old. I worked with the white peoples when I was ten or twelve. It don't make no difference if I'm a black boy and you're a white boy. You see, back in those days if you come over here, and you and me go out in the yard and start playin'—we get to fightin'. My momma would whup you. . . . Now, if you put your hands on a man's child like that, first thing he'll say is, "I'll kill you."

Another cropper's wife in her sixties said she could not remember "any trouble in our neighborhood between blacks and whites. We lived next door to some white ladies and we used to run back and forth borrowing some sugar or some salt. We would sit at the table and eat together, always would joke together." But then she added, "The white ladies always called my parents 'uncle' and 'auntie'—just ol' slavery talk."

A variety of motivations prompt croppers to move. One woman said, "I don't stay anywhere too long. If you stay on a job too long, people'll think they own you." Another family "usually move every year or so" because they "get tired of the same man."

> We do all the work and he gets half. He just sits there doing nothing. They try to tend it all themselves. They want all the crops. . . . They're so greedy. . . . When you pay him for what you owe him that leaves you with nothin'. You go away and make the best you can. And if you're going to farm with him another year, in March you go to him and borrow some more money until September 1. It takes all you can make to pay him. He don't care how you live, just as long as you make another crop.

A mother of four children said that every year, come January, they have the same thing—nothing. "You're never completely out, yet you were never rising so high. It's a way to keep from dyin'."

Incidents in which a landlord tries to run a cropper off the farm in order to take over his crop are common. There is the case of George Wicker, a black cropper working for a white female landlord, who fought back in the North Carolina courts when he learned of proceedings initiated against him.

> My mother got sick and I needed $100 to take her to Duke [University] Hospital . . . . The landlord said, "I ain't got no $100." Then, I asked her son, and he said, "No, I ain't got no $100; what in the world are you worrying about; she's gonna die anyhow." I started crying and said I see you all won't help me, but you want me to work. I took a walk and the lady comes and says, "If you quit me, I'll sell that acre of 'bacco I gave you. I'll spend every penny of it to see you in the Army. I will have you put on the chain gang."

Wicker left the farm and found an employer who would pay him $45 a week and give him the $100 advance. He took his mother to Duke Hospital, where she was diagnosed as having cancer. Meanwhile, his former landlord had filed suit against him for $115. Wicker continues:

> We went to court and I lost. I was sentenced to six months on the roads. My lawyer asked me if I wanted to appeal the case to Raleigh. He said, "If they find you guilty, you're liable to get two years. What do you want to do?" "Let's go to Raleigh with it 'cause if I get two years, at least, I'll have tried to help myself . . . ."
> [A few days before the court hearing] the lawyer asked me how long I'd been working with her. "Ever since the first of the year," I said. "I went there and helped break all the land. I helped plant all the crop. I stayed there and layed by the corn, layed by the 'bacco, helped topsoil before I left."
> [In court] it was a bloody battle. She said I was the worst black man she had ever seen. . . . When the chief juror stood up there I was scared to death. . . . He said, "Your honor, we find him not guilty." Then, the judge said she had to pay for my labor. He really gave it to her. "You owe this boy," the judge said. "You ought to be ashamed of yourself." Then, he said she had to pay me $940.50. You could hear her yell from here down to that store yonder [about half a mile]. She said if I was ever on her land again, she'd shoot me like a rabbit.

Dotting the countryside are a multitude of churches and grocery store—service stations. It is not difficult to tell the black churches from the white ones. The largest black church in the county is Jones Chapel, a Baptist church with a congregation of between 75 and 100 members. The preaching Sunday is the first one of the month; on the other three Sundays the members hold services without a minister. The chapel is a white-painted concrete building; the paint is peeling, and the wood doors are rotting. Behind the church is a graveyard covered by mud and clay. There are also two outhouses with the words "Men" and "Women" spray-painted in large black letters.

During the 1930s and the 1940s nearly everybody used to go to church. In fact, back then the community as a whole revolved around the church schedule. A prominent black minister in the county who is about seventy years old said the 1930s were "a time in which the church was all in all. If a person was a Christian, he'd go to church. If a person wanted religion he'd go to church. If he wanted a wife he'd go to church. If they wanted a drink of liquor, they'd come to church." Outside the church, family structures and kinship patterns remain strong even when family members have migrated north to urban areas. Many return to the South several times a year, often for the holidays, usually when there is no work.

Sharecroppers, like many others, are confused by the ironies of attitudes and actions displayed by some local whites. One asked, "How can he look at you smiling, say how do you do . . . and then go do something like burn a cross. It's terrible how people's minds can get so warped, crippled up that they think they are doing what is right when they get out there killing somebody."

Back in the 1960s, because they could not understand, there was a great fear of what might happen. A minister described the impotence of his church in fighting the Ku Klux Klan, the school boards, and the town council. Making it into an allegory, he said, "The rats got together and said that in order that the cat won't catch all of us, let's put a bell on the cat and then we'll all know when he's coming. All of the rats decided it was a good idea. But when one of them had to bell the cat—well, everything came to a standstill."

Even today, black sharecroppers are fearful of the unknown in the white community: "The KKK is still here. People think it's gone, but it ain't. You know that mess is poppin' up all over the news lately. If something come up right now, I believe where it would be black against white, and they had a whole lot of trouble, they'd start up again. I doubt if they'd wear their masks. They don't care." Memories are not so quickly erased. Croppers remember the young black adolescent who was hung for "going with a white woman." They remember the fire bombings of the black stores and speakeasies and how the newspaper implied that blacks were responsible for their own deaths and destruction. They remember the Klansmen shooting into the homes of black families who wanted to send their children to predominantly white schools. "You still don't trust yourself to go in the front door, if you don't know the place. Now, it's all right in Louisburg because we know everybody. Now, you take my husband, we don't go out places to eat because he don't know whether blacks are allowed. . . . You see, he is so uncertain of it, that he just doesn't want to be bothered with it."

Many of the sharecroppers forced off the land in the last twenty years remain in Franklin County seeking work as day-laborers and at other odd jobs. Most of them never find stable employment; the most they can hope for is a job during the tobacco harvest and during the peak periods of the mill industry. They are stranded with their families in the same run-down houses that they have always lived in. The fate of these tenants presents a Catch-22 dilemma: while at last they are free of a landlord to exploit them, they are also without a landlord to feed and house them.

CASH-TENANTS: BETTER HOMES AND GARDENS

In nearly every case, homes of tenant farmers are important symbols of class differences. In Franklin County, one new house in eight was financed through the Farmers' Home Administration (FmHA). Most cash-tenants, it was found, secured loans from the FmHA and commerical lending institutions. All of the cash-tenants included in this study lived in recently built homes, financed with borrowed money.

These new homes, usually of brick although sometimes of clapboard, have storm windows, doors that lock, shutters, flower boxes, and impeccably painted veneers. They are quite unlike the southern stereotype: the old box-frame, two-story structure where chickens scurry under and about a dilapidated porch. Behind the house is a half-acre or an acre garden, barren in the winter, teeming in the summer with tomatoes, cucumbers, white potatoes, lima beans, okra, collard greens, cabbage, string beans, black-eyed peas, and grasshoppers. Nearby, old rotted structures are the refuge of hogs, chickens, and rabbits. Some renting families have their own smokehouses, hung full of "curing" pork joints. Barely visible inside the dark gaping entrances of buck barns and old sheds are the bright green tractors and the enormous combines—the mechanical primers ready to pluck the tobacco leaves—while ancient wagons, forgotten plows, churns, and occasionally an old car rust beneath the abandoned ruins, the refuse of generations of farm work and living.

Despite all of the signs of a better life, there looms the oppression of perpetual debt. These cash-tenants are proud of their homes, yet they look forward anxiously to the day when payments will be complete. "All farmers work on borrowed money. All they want to do is have one year when they don't have to borrow. Each year is a make-or-break one; farmin' is a gamble. . . . Lots of pressure—you could lose everything in a bad year, you have so much invested."

Despite these pressures, and the vagaries of farm work, there is a deep bond between the renter and his land. One cash-tenant, an insurance salesman for ten years before returning to farming, explained his preference for working the land rather than "public work" in this way: "I wanted to farm so bad; I was working *and* farming. As long as I was a worker, I would never be anything but a worker." Occasionally, cash-tenants hold "public work" jobs to supplement their incomes from farming, jobs as sawyers, mechanics, carpenters, and janitors. Many of the cash-tenants talked of their sense of freedom in farming and the importance of being entirely responsible both for themselves and their families.

Typically, the cash-tenant is white. Like landowners who farm, renters think of themselves as part of the owner/operator elite. Most of these tenants are fortunate in that they can read, but many would like to continue their education. One renter lamented the fact that he was taken out of school to work in the fields during the eighth grade. Both his wife and two children have finished high school. His father, he recalled, could not read.

Usually, marriages in cash-tenant households are long lasting and husbands and wives mutually supportive. Women tend to marry soon after graduating from high school; their husbands are generally older and less well educated. Divorce is permissible, but not "in this house." Most often, women and children defer to the "man-boss"—his word is law. Yet, when he is out of earshot, the wife and children quickly become more candid and often express divergent opinions. The women are full-time workers in the home; their day starts with breakfast, usually around 5:00 A.M. In summer, they run errands for their husbands in the mornings and provide box-type lunches at noon. Simply clothed, they wear almost no makeup, jewelry, or other adornments. Women's liberation does not have much of a constituency among these women or their husbands.

Renters realize that they have benefited greatly from many of the recent societal changes, yet they are troubled. They remember their childhoods as "peaceful, lovin', happy times" when everybody got along well. Now, it seems, life is busier and less certain. They say that it was easy to get workers in the 1940s. Now, "it's hard to find *good* day-laborers. They will only work on Wednesday and Thursday. . . . It didn't used to be like that. . . . Those welfare families don't really try." Cash-tenants were usually unaware of, and would have been unswayed by, evidence that only 31 percent of those eligible for social welfare services in Franklin County actually participated in such programs (Hoffman 1977:2–3).

In their eyes, the greatest change thus far is the integration of schools and public places of business. The wife of one renter recalls that originally she had been in favor of integrating buses and restaurants. That was "until one day when I sat down at a lunch counter next to a black man. I didn't know what to do; I felt uncomfortable. I had to leave." Then, she added with a nervous laugh, "You have to get used to those things." During her childhood, she once called a black man "Mister." "Well, everybody laughed [but] I thought it was the right thing to do." Her children say that she was reared as a racist; she denies this, but then wonders out loud whether it might not have been implicit in her upbringing.

While cash-tenants are more politically aware than other tenant groups, they seldom vote. They are cautious and skeptical. "I used to think the president could be effective. Now, I don't think he is. Congress should do it, but won't." By not voting, some of them believe that they are resisting, that they are showing their disapproval of government and of integration. Uniformly, they feel that the quality of education in the public schools has declined in the ten years since integration was started.

Sunday mornings are still for Sunday school. Many of these families go to large Southern Baptist churches close to their homes. One such church, Mt. Zion Baptist, stands on a hill overlooking the homes of these tenants. The church is white from its clapboard to its congregation. "Colored don't come here, and we don't go there," was one comment. The steeple rises high in the sky; the inside space is small and crowded with many older faces on Sunday mornings. Everyone agrees that church-going used to be more important. However, now that traveling has become easier, people find other places to go. Some simply stay home and watch television.

Nearly all of the children of these tenants have completed high school. Most of those who remain in the county move closer to the towns of Louisburg and Franklinton. Rarely do they farm. They prefer the security of a weekly or a biweekly paycheck—something their parents eschewed.

Generally conservative in their dress, their actions, and their politics, the renting class espouses a deep sense of patriotism. They hold fast to traditional values of hard work, Christianity, and racial solidarity. They are quick to protect their interests, particularly when it affects the farm or the family.

While many cash-tenants seem satisfied with their circumstances, they feel threatened by the future. The changes that they have witnessed in the last thirty years confuse them. Over the years they have watched small farmers like themselves, throughout North Carolina, lose their fields to corporate enterprises. And they wonder how much time is left.

CONCLUSIONS

Since the 1960s, the tenant farmer population has decreased to the point where the system's prolonged existence seems highly unlikely. Threatened by the rapid growth of corporate farming and related technologies, tenant farming has been all but eliminated as a profitable financial or political enterprise.

Yet many displaced sharecroppers remain in the South, working as day-laborers and in other low levels of employment, usually within a few miles of where they last tended land. Outside of the peak season, the day-laborer is dismissed and forgotten by the community. What is perhaps worse, his existence is not accounted for by agricultural-census takers; he is neglected by government officials, turned aside by landowners, and stereotyped as "lazy" and a welfare recipient by the general public. None of the five sharecroppers interviewed for this study farm any longer. Two have retired, and the others were unable to secure contracts.

The future of the cash-tenant is less bleak. Over the last two decades, the cash-tenant population has grown in proportion to other forms of tenancy. In areas where small farms survive, cash-tenants are considered an asset to busy landowners. Moreover, because of his greater economic resources, the cash-tenant has been able to adapt to a changing system of farming. Demographic data indicate that tenancy in the late 1970s was increasingly dominated by white farmers between the ages of 34 and 54.

However, the children of these cash-tenants, both black and white, are fleeing the farm. Increasingly, they enjoy, and are now exposed to, greater opportunities. The sharecroppers' children, most of whom are now adults, see little future for themselves on the farm and consequently pursue employment in low-level, nonfarm vocations.

Economic and social mobility is still possible within the ranks, although it seems primarily limited to whites. Above all, the white population has been increasingly responsible for transforming tenancy from share-crop to cash-rent, from exploitation to independence, from low-income to middle-income status, from black hands to white hands, and from small-time farming to medium-size farming.

NOTES

Many people were indispensable to me throughout the term of this project. At Duke University, William H. Chafe, Marsha J. Darling, Bruce Payne, and Carol B. Stack were helpful in so many professional and personal ways that I can only say thanks. I am grateful to my friends Linda Daniel, Cindy Frisch, and Richard Petrow for all their guidance, patience, and love. And then there were the tenant farmers of Franklin County who shared with me and helped me to share in some very memorable ways.

The research for this paper was done under the aegis of the Duke University Oral History Program.

1. This was the last US agriculture census to provide figures broken down by category of tenant farmer. Figures from my study showed no significant change from the census.

2. Interview with staff, United States Department of Agriculture, in Louisburg, North Carolina, January 1978.

3. Quotations from tenant farmers were elicited in visits and interviews in Franklin County, North Carolina, from December 1977 through March 1978. Unattributed quotes and pseudonyms have been used, since some interviewees asked that their names not be revealed.

REFERENCES

Hoffman, Steven J., 1977. *Food Stamps and the North Carolina Economy* (Charlotte: North Carolina Hunger Coalition).

Myrdal, Gunnar, 1944. *An American Dilemma: The Negro Problem and Modern Democracy* (New York: Harper and Row).

Powdermaker, Hortense, 1939. *After Freedom: A Cultural Study in the Deep South* (New York: Viking Press).

US Bureau of the Census, 1964. *Agriculture Census of 1964*, vol. 1, pt. 26 (Washington, D.C.: US Government Printing Office).

US Bureau of the Census, 1977. Farming Populations of the U.S.: 1976. *Current Population Reports*, P-27, no. 49, December (Washington, D.C.: US Government Printing Office).

Appalachian Families, Landownership, and Public Policy

PATRICIA D. BEAVER

From the end of the Civil War until recently, rural southern Appalachian mountain communities have been defined by their relative isolation from economic and communication centers. Subsistence farming has been a primary economic activity, supplemented by a variety of other activities—such as timbering, mining, cash cropping, and temporary out-migration for work—as they have become available. Although permanent wage labor is a relatively new phenomenon in the mountains, becoming important to the majority of the labor force only after the 1940s, labor diversification and the exploitation of a variety of economic sources are not new. Historically these diverse income sources have helped the family to survive.

Agriculture has historically been the basis of the rural mountain family economy. While this remains true for a few, most families now rely on agriculture only as a supplement to other income sources. Some families simply raise a garden and keep a few chickens, while a few raise livestock and a variety of cash crops as their sole income source. Burley tobacco proves a most dependable agricultural income source for many.

Permanent wage labor is an important income source, although it is only one of many potential income sources. As the local economy changes, permanent wage labor is becoming increasingly important. However, the subsistence agriculture orientation still dominates much community interaction and family organization.

The southern Appalachian rural community is built on a legacy of extensive, overlapping kin networks. The family network is the community, and family identity is synonymous with place. Family, and thus community identity, is bound up with community historical events and rootedness in the land. The agricultural heritage, though vastly diminished in importance in recent years, provides the context for family and community relationships, despite the domination of local economies by light industry and varieties of "public work."

Because of various historical processes, discussed below, single industry domination of local economies is characteristic of the entire southern Appalachian region. The timber industry was followed by mineral development, tourism, and the advent of secondary industries such as small-scale manufacturing and textiles. While the resource industries have been characterized by boom-and-bust economic cycles, the resort industry and manufacturing industries are beset by frequent layoffs, low wages, minimal upward mobility, and few if any benefits. At the same time, recreation development and resource utilization have intensified land speculation and have led to inflationary land prices and high taxes. The single industries—most notably recreation, natural resource (primarily mineral and timber), and textile industries— through their ownership of land and lack of competition, place various inhibitions on individual mobility and pressures on the economics of landownership. Rising land prices, in turn, are affecting the viability of agriculture, the possibility of land acquisition and ownership, the availability of housing, and thus the very structure of the rural family and community. Changes in landownership, and increasing control of land by nonlocal corporate and public interests, necessitate examination of the fundamental public policy issues that affect the rural mountain family.

By the turn of this century, the southern Appalachian region was a well-populated, productive region of the nation, with a complex rural society and an economy geared primarily toward subsistence farming and cash crops. Following the Civil War, however, the region experienced a certain relative isolation from communication centers and trade, as well as limited availability of revenues for education, roads, and other communication systems. The Civil War had been a time of great internal division in southern Appalachia. Many counties and families were split as strong Confederacy sentiment ran into conflict with abolitionist and isolationist points of view. Pro-Unionism in the mountains did not go unnoticed by piedmont—Confederacy—portions of the Appalachian states; one result of the postwar legislative control by nonmountain sections of Appalachian states was the virtual cutoff of funds for roads and schools to the mountains. The states' limited funds would not have stretched far into the mountains anyway, but because they resented pro-Union "traitors" in the mountain sections, those in control of state funds did not feel particularly compelled to share the limited wealth.

Around the turn of the century, the natural resources of the southern Appalachians, particularly timber and minerals, were discovered by the outside society. Speculation in mineral and timber lands, begun much earlier in the region's history, intensified during this time. Between 1910 and 1920, the railroad opened up the mountains to commerce in a major way, and the industrial appetites of a rapidly industrializing society began gnawing at the natural resources of the region. The availability of a cheap labor force began to attract industries to the mountain fringe areas. Between 1900 and 1930, over six hundred company towns sprang up in the southern Appalachians (Eller 1978),

drawing mountain families from the farm and into factory towns. The resulting speculation and exploitation of the region's resources provided new work
alternatives for rural mountain families, while developing into boom-and-bust
economic cycles.

By the 1940s the population in the region had reached its highest concentration; but as the local agricultural economy began to decline and the cost of
living began to rise, economic growth in urban industrial centers began to
draw migrants out of the region in increasing numbers. World War II saw the
beginning of the large-scale migration of mountain people out of Appalachia
to northern industrial centers and the depopulation of the rural communities;
consistent with national trends, this process has halted and begun to reverse
itself only in the past ten years. Between 1940 and 1960 approximately three
million people left Appalachia.

During the post–Civil War period, then, Appalachia was relatively isolated
from development trends occurring in the nonmountain portions of the eastern states and, further, was relatively isolated from revenue sources to support
public education, transportation, and other public facilities. It was during this
period, however, that mainstream society made two major "discoveries" in
the region. Industrial and commercial interests discovered the region's vast
store of natural resources, and mainstream America discovered "hillbilly"
culture. The local color movement in American fiction, always on the alert for
the "quaint" and the "curious," first dramatized for a new American middle-
class audience the "otherness," the distinctiveness, of Appalachia's people as
somehow set apart from American society as a whole (Shapiro 1978). The
local color writers had a significant influence on the mission movement that
entered southern Appalachia around the turn of the century. A major thrust of
the mission movement was the development of educational opportunities, and
a major premise, stemming from the local color perspective, was that the
quaint folk of the mountains could achieve unity with American society as a
whole only if educated away from their traditions (Shapiro 1978). The modern
educational system in Appalachia thus has its post–Civil War origins in an
educational philosophy dominated by nonregional goals and priorities.

More recent visions of Appalachia by mainstream society have been sold
by the media through "Li'l Abner and Daisy Mae," "The Beverly Hill-
billies," "Snuffy Smith," "Green Acres," "Hee Haw," and *Deliverance*. The
images portrayed are none too flattering, but they nevertheless have been
bought and sold.

As for the social sciences, one of the major statements on the region remains Jack Weller's *Yesterday's People* (1965), an analysis of an eastern Kentucky community written during the mid-1960s and firmly grounded in the
"culture of poverty" model. The basic assumption of Weller's theoretical perspective is that of the deficiency of Appalachian culture when compared with

mainstream society. Weller compared Appalachian rural culture with an urban ideal, and where the two differed, he found Appalachia sadly lacking. Since the 1960s both the social sciences and Mr. Weller have changed. Weller labeled mountain people fatalistic in 1965; in 1978, after living and working in the culture, seeing his own bright hopes dashed by the rapacious demands of an extractive industry, and watching agency funds dry up, he notes that the people are realistic in accepting those things that powerful political, economic, and environmental circumstances have proven cannot be changed (Jack Weller, personal communication). The unfortunate part of Weller's early work is that it provided a model with which social scientists and agents of public policy are reluctant to part.

The development of a national image of Appalachia as a region set apart from the mainstream—forgotten, lost, and deprived of the bounty in America—provided legitimacy for several kinds of intervention. On the one hand, agents of social and cultural change reiterated and publicized this image in order to gather support—financial and social—for the establishment of educational institutions that would correct the inadequacies. On the other hand, business and government interests were legitimized in their accelerated movement to control the region's natural resources and labor force.

Social scientists also accepted the basic assumptions of the distinctiveness, quaintness, and inadequacy of Appalachian culture in their approach to the region. From early attempts to discover America's frontier in Appalachia, through studies of Appalachian genetic deterioration and the subculture of poverty, the basic premise remains that the region is set apart, deprived, and in need of help for change.

Although consistently involved in the variety of economic activities that were available, the rural mountain family was traditionally patterned around a continuing reliance on subsistence agriculture. Despite a rapid decline in the number of farms, the amount of land in farms, and the number of people involved in farming, agricultural activities—including gardening and the raising of limited numbers of cash crops, livestock, or burley tobacco—are supportive of the family system and the family economy. The rural mountain family finds continuity, stability, and identity through the values embodied in land and community.

The nuclear family, formed by marriage and traditionally through elopement, has been a quasi-independent economic and social unit, with a separate household, separate household economy, and primary responsibility for the socialization of children (Beaver 1976). The nuclear family, however, is firmly grounded in an extended family network; this network of related families is often residentially clustered near the parental homeplace. Members of discrete households rely on each other for labor, financial support, assistance in large cooperative activities, and psychological support.

The frequent unpredictability of the economy, the environment (where flooding or winter storms can isolate communities), and service facilities (especially health care) has necessitated nuclear family self-reliance, independence, and creative individual problem-solving; it also has required cooperation among groups of people in large-scale activities and in times of crisis. The mountain family is rooted in the land. Land is symbolically associated with family and has often been in a family for several generations. Landownership traditionally has provided a margin of economic stability and embodies family solidarity and unity. Land usually has been acquired through inheritance—or purchased for a nominal fee—from elderly relatives, although it would not be passed on to the younger generation before the older folks died. The elderly, by retaining ownership of land and residing in a separate household (though in close proximity to helping kin), thereby retained a degree of power and authority within the family structure.

Agriculture has been a significant factor in the economies of most southern Appalachian rural communities, although recent changes in landownership and land use have threatened the viability of agriculture in major ways. While the decline in agriculture in the mountains is consistent with the national trend, it has been accelerated by dramatic changes in regional landownership and land prices resulting from resource and recreational development.

Resort land speculation and development had begun to a limited degree during the late nineteenth and early twentieth centuries in exclusive resort areas like Roan Mountain, Blowing Rock, Linville, Little Switzerland, and Hendersonville. During the 1960s the mountains witnessed the rapid acceleration of land speculation and the development of a full-scale tourist industry. With the new development, land prices began skyrocketing as investment values reflected heavy market activity.

With respect to recreational development in Watauga County, North Carolina, for example, land speculation for second-home and resort development during the last fifteen to twenty years has caused a dramatic increase in land values and in taxes (Moretz 1979). Between 1961 and 1974, the county experienced a 300 percent increase in the tax base; the value of real estate nearly doubled—from $320 million to $522 million—from the previous tax revaluation to the recent revaluation (Moretz 1979:57). The increasing land prices are affecting local agriculture in several ways. The high cost of land keeps many prospective farmers out of agriculture because they cannot afford to purchase the land initially. Particularly for young families who have not established equities, the option of farming, or even of purchasing land for housing, is practically nonexistent. In addition, unless a family owns land "or inherits it at reasonable costs, it would be impossible to make a farm bought at inflated prices economically viable" (Moretz 1979:57). The high property taxes, reflecting inflated land values, make it "difficult for smaller farms to remain economically viable . . . sometimes forcing families to sell part or all of their land." Land speculation therefore becomes "punitive to farmers and others who want to keep their land. . . . Farmers and local people should not be penalized or forced to subsidize the recreation industry, when such development is forcing some people off their land" (Moretz 1979:59–60).

Branscombe and Matthews (1974:124) noted that recreational and resort development had "driven the price of marginal farm and timber land from a low of $100 an acre to a whopping $1,000 an acre in a half decade. Rough, undeveloped land in Macon County, North Carolina, goes for as high as $5,000 per acre, and near the second-home center of Highlands, it reaches $20,000 if water and sewers are available. In Madison County, which has few developments, land is already selling for $1,000 an acre, 'and that's for straight up-and-down land,' says one resident. A three-quarter-acre lot in highly developed Watauga County can go for $6,000 and still be considered 'a darn good buy.' " Needless to say, even these figures have altered dramatically in the ensuing six years.

The direct effect of inflated land prices on local property taxes is clear. The demand for local services and facilities on the part of the resort/recreational industry exceeds their contribution to the tax base: "The long-time resident is forced to subsidize the very developers who would run him off his land" (Branscombe and Matthews 1974:128).

The issue of taxation becomes intensified in those counties where extensive tracts of land are publicly owned, and a major factor in the land-use issue is the federal ownership of land. The United States Forest Service, for example, is exempt from most local taxation. Local landowners must therefore bear a major burden for public services—such as roads and public facilities—even though the bulk of land may be outside-owned and -controlled; the very existence of Forest Service land attracts multitudes of outsiders to the county. Further, local property taxes are generally higher in counties with extensive federal landholdings than for other counties in the state. For example, in Swain County, North Carolina, various federal agencies control over 80 percent of the county's land, or 272,978 of the 339,200 available acres (Efird 1979:63); the Great Smoky Mountains National Park leads with 63.1 percent of the county's land. Of the land not controlled by the federal government, corporate outside interests own approximately one quarter, while nonlocal private owners also own a significant number of acres (Efird 1979:63).

Lack of available land means limited, if any, productive capacity and development potential for the local economy. New industries are not attracted to the county because of lack of available land. The existing industries—as elsewhere in the rural mountain counties—are the low-wage furniture and textile industries. Poverty rates in Swain County are high, with per capita personal income in 1977 at $4,368 (Efird 1979). "Low income figures result in a population dependent on public assistance, and in Swain County, 25.8% of all families have incomes below poverty level" (Efird 1979:64). The high percentage of publicly owned land further complicates the problem of low income and the county's abilities to provide services because the land is tax-exempt—only 18 percent of the land in the county is taxable (Efird 1979:64).

The US Forest Service is the largest single landowner in Appalachia, controlling nearly 5,400,000 acres in eight states (Kahn 1974). In 1972 the average payment to local counties by the Forest Service was "less than 14 cents an acre, and well under 10% of what the property taxes alone would have been if the land were still in private hands" (Kahn 1974:134). Although federally owned lands are tax-exempt, the Forest Service does pay a small amount to local counties from a fund authorized by the 1911 Weeks Act, which authorized 25 percent of the revenues acquired by the Forest Service to be paid back to the counties for public schools and roads (Kahn 1974). The Forest Service's income is generated primarily from the sale of timber—mostly pulpwood—and in southern Appalachia the amount cut is dependent on Forest Service decisions; revenues to the counties are therefore minimal and unpredictable, varying widely from county to county and state to state. "The average payment per acre for all National Forests in all states was 58 cents. The average payment per acre for all Appalachian National Forests was 13.5 cents" (Kahn 1974:135).

Most dramatically affected by the presence of the Forest Service are those fourteen Appalachian counties in which the Forest Service owns more than 40 percent of the land. In 1970, for these fourteen counties, the average population was low—less than 9,000—and the average poverty rate was 29.2 percent; between 1940 and 1970 they had lost 13.2 percent of their populations (Kahn 1974). "These counties are affected not only by revenue loss, lack of public services, high poverty incidence and outmigration rates, but—to add insult to injury—by local property taxes that are significantly higher than those in counties without National Forest lands . . . the effective tax rate for these counties is on the average 15% higher than the average effective tax rate for the state . . . and in at least one case, Fanin County, Georgia, was the highest in the state" (Kahn 1974:136).

The small family farm is currently supported by local industry. The dairyman's wife, the cattleman's wife, and the subsistence farmer's wife do shift work. The farmer himself is a trucker, or works in town, farming in the evenings and on weekends. The small family farm cannot support the family, and major income supplements must come from other sources. Of the few fulltime farmers in Watauga County, North Carolina, two-thirds work at another job on a part-time basis, "and only one-third produce more than $2500 per year" (Moretz 1979:58). These other sources of income, however, are often long distances from the community; they are seasonal with frequent layoffs, as in the resort or building industries; or they are low-wage, nonunion with little upward mobility and few benefits, as in the numerous secondary industries found throughout the mountain region. The quality of life available through maintaining control over the family farm is of great value to many rural families, and the family will make tremendous sacrifices in order to hold on to land. What are the consequences, however, of a layoff, or a firing? The answer is demoralization of the family, a forced sale of land; and consequent increasing dependence of the family on "public work" or on public assistance.

Further, public assistance policy, when it requires disposal of land, means permanent alienation from the land and permanent dependence. The eligibility requirements of Aid to Families with Dependent Children (AFDC) exempt only the applicant's home and one acre of land, and then only if the applicant resides there. Any land owned above that one acre is counted as reserve, and the allowable reserve—including other resources such as an automobile—is limited to $1,000 for one person, $1,100 for two, and an additional $50 for each extra person. Thus, AFDC virtually eliminates eligibility on the part of families who own a quantity of land. In those families for whom AFDC may be the only means—even though temporary—for survival, the deeding or sale of existing land is a necessity. The immediate consequences of utilizing AFDC to support the family may be the family's temporary sustenance; the long-term consequences are increasing dependence on agency support and alienation from agriculture as an economic alternative.

Although the Food Stamp program was in the past restrictive with regard to landownership, it now grants eligibility despite ownership of land, with some restrictions. Participants may own any amount of land of any value as long as it is contiguous to their residence.

The southern Appalachian region presents a unique picture for the rest of the nation with regard to landownership, resource exploitation, and public policy. Wealth in timber, a variety of minerals, a rural small-farm population that is a potentially cheap labor force, abundant water, and great natural scenic beauty create a setting for massive industrial exploitation. The interplay between the vast wealth of natural resources, industrialization, and the existence of a basically rural agricultural population sets the stage for dramatic exploitation, outside control over much of the resources, and the constant disruption of the rural context.

The development and elaboration of the resort industry has resulted in a shifting tax base, inflationary land values, and stepped-up resource acquisition by outside corporate and noncorporate financial/investment interests. Combined with the decreasing viability of small-scale agriculture, all of these factors have mitigated against both the viability of the small farm and the ownership of land at all.

Public policy with regard to Appalachia has been urban policy, and the issue of landownership is critical, having ramifications in health care, child care, housing, and transportation. Ownership of the land has provided social stability, cultural continuity, and economic viability for rural Appalachia throughout the entire history of the region. With regard to the alienation of land from the rural family, what was for a time an option has now become for many a mandate. The stability, continuity, and vitality of the rural mountain family has rested in the land. Landownership is becoming increasingly impossible, but the economic alternatives that would enhance family stability are not evident.

REFERENCES

Beaver, Patricia D., 1976. *Symbols and Social Organization in an Appalachian Mountain Community* (Ph.D. diss., Duke University).

Branscome, Jim, and Peggy Matthews, 1974. Selling the Mountains. *Southern Exposure* 2:122–29.

Efird, Cathy M., 1979. Public Land Ownership: Its Impact on Swain County, North Carolina. In *Citizen Participation in Rural Land Use Planning for the Tennessee Valley*, Lindsay Jones, ed. (Nashville: Agricultural Marketing Project), pp. 62–66.

Eller, Ronald, 1978. Industrialization and Social Change in Appalachia, 1880–1930. In *Colonialism in Modern America: The Appalachian Case*, Helen Lewis, Linda Johnson, and Donald Askins, eds. (Boone, N.C.: Appalachian Consortium Press), pp. 35–46.

Kahn, Si, 1974. The Government's Private Forests. *Southern Exposure* 2:132–44.

Moretz, Albert Ray, 1979. The Impact of Recreational Development on Agriculture in Watauga County. In *Citizen Participation in Rural Land Use Planning for the Tennessee Valley*, Lindsay Jones, ed. (Nashville: Agricultural Marketing Project), pp. 56–61.

Shapiro, Henry, 1978. *Appalachia on Our Mind* (Chapel Hill: University of North Carolina Press).

Weller, Jack, 1965. *Yesterday's People: Life in Contemporary Appalachia* (Lexington: University of Kentucky Press).

The Contributors

ALLEN BATTEAU is an assistant professor of social science and anthropology at Michigan State University. His interest in Appalachia began in 1968 when he did a semester of undergraduate field study at Pikeville College in eastern Kentucky. This college, he states in a recent paper, was "the only college in America in the 1960s where the student demonstrations protested the administration's communistic activity." This, and similar ironies, have led him to return to the mountains several times, in 1972, 1973–75, and 1978, to conduct further fieldwork. He is the author of several articles and papers on Appalachian kinship, politics, and culture.

PATRICIA D. BEAVER spent her early years in a mill village in the Blue Ridge mountains of western North Carolina. At eighteen she left the mountains to be educated at Duke University, received her Ph.D. in 1976, and returned to study the complexity of life back in the hills. She is director of the Center for Appalachian Studies and associate professor of anthropology at Appalachian State University in Boone, North Carolina. She has written several articles on the Appalachian family, and is actively involved in research in Appalachia on sex roles, social organization, land tenure, and public policy issues.

KAY YOUNG DAY is a doctoral student at Rutgers University. Her interest in the South and in the Sea Islands began as an undergraduate at Georgia State University in Atlanta, where she was born and raised. She began her research with the people of Mt. Pleasant in 1971. Kay and Greg Day lived in a Mt. Pleasant black community for a year and a half documenting traditional material culture under a grant from the Smithsonian Institution. Since entering graduate school in 1972, her research in the Sea Islands has focused on social history and kin and community organization. She is completing her dissertation on the role of kin and community in a changing economy.

JOHN A. FORREST converted an amateur interest in traditional English folk music into a profession as an anthropologist. While a student at Oxford, he supplemented his student grant by singing traditional English folk music and later began collecting songs directly from the traditional singers themselves. He later undertook graduate work in anthropology at the University of North Carolina, Chapel Hill, where he had completed an M.A. in folklore in 1977. By the time he began fieldwork in a small fishing community in the swamplands of northeastern North Carolina, the scope of his interests had broadened from British folk songs that had been brought to the United States to the totality of the aesthetic realm of folk communities. The topic of his doctoral dissertation, completed in 1980, was the aesthetics of this northeastern North Carolina fishing community.

BRUCE T. GRINDAL, associate professor of anthropology at Florida State University, was born in 1940 in Geneva, Illinois, received his B.A. from Northwestern University (1963) and his Ph.D. from Indiana University (1969). His research interests include education and social change and the study of religion. He has conducted fieldwork in Ghana, West Africa (1966–68), and among religious groups in the South. He is particularly interested in the forms of religious expression found among black Americans. His major publications include *Growing Up in Two Worlds* and, with Dennis Warren, *Essays in Humanistic Anthropology*. He is also the founder and current editor of the *Anthropology and Humanism Quarterly*.

B. LISA GRÖGER was born in Czechoslovakia and grew up in a Bavarian peasant village. She later lived in England and France before coming to the United States, where she earned her Ph.D. in anthropology from Columbia University in 1979. Intrigued by academicians' interest in the peasant life from which she had worked so hard to escape, she conducted her doctoral research in a French peasant community. She is a postdoctoral fellow at the Center for the Study of Aging and Human Development at the Duke University Medical Center. Her recently begun study of rural aging in North Carolina brought her in contact with small farmers whose lives in many ways resemble the lives of their European counterparts.

ROBERT L. HALL is an instructor of history at Florida State University, where he is currently a doctoral candidate. He is a specialist in American history with a background in African history. His research interests include black history, race relations, and the role of religion among black Southerners. Hall received a Whitney Young Fellowship in 1978, and was a visiting fellow in 1980 at the Center for the Study of Civil Rights and Race Relations at Duke University. He has published papers on the Student Nonviolent Coordinating Committee, minority students, slave religion, and black migration. He is writing a history of religion among blacks in Florida from the sixteenth to the nineteenth centuries.

YVONNE V. JONES, assistant professor of anthropology and Pan African studies at the University of Louisville, received the Ph.D. degree in 1975 from the American University in Washington, D.C. Her primary interests are political change and political ecology, Afro-American kinship, and urban anthropology. Her major research has focused on socioeconomic and political change in the American South, and family structure among rural blacks. Most recently she has been interested in federal housing policies and neighborhood integration.

SYDNEY NATHANS is associate professor of history at Duke University. He trained in nineteenth-century United States history at the Johns Hopkins University, and has published a book on Daniel Webster. He and his interests have migrated to the South, and he trespasses regularly in the domain of anthropology. His current work focuses on the history, from the mid-nineteenth century to the present, of three related black rural settlements that had their origins as slave communities.

JAMES L. PEACOCK is professor of anthropology at the University of North Carolina, Chapel Hill. His primary interests are psychological and symbolic anthropology, with particular emphasis on the ideological dimensions of modernization. He has done fieldwork in Indonesia, Singapore, and North Carolina and is the author of numerous publications, including *The Human Direction* (with A. Thomas Kirsch), a text in cultural anthropology.

STEVEN PETROW, writer-journalist, has worked in and studied southern migrant farmworker communities during the last four years. During this time, he has become increasingly interested in the racial and economic status of tenant farmers, the South's other historic agricultural labor. He has also written about Haitian refugees and Jamaican immigrants. He is a graduate student in American history at the University of California, Berkeley.

CAROL B. STACK is director of the Center for the Study of the Family and the State at Duke University, where she is associate professor of public policy and anthropology. The author of *All Our Kin: Strategies for Survival in a Black Community*, she is completing a monograph on family policy in the United States. She received her Ph.D. from the University of Illinois in 1972. Her research combines a background in philosophy and ethics with an interest in policy and advocacy. She is now engaged in research on return migration to the South.

BRETT SUTTON came to anthropology with a background in humanistic studies that includes a B.A. in English from the University of Illinois at Urbana

(1970) and an M.A. in folklore from the University of North Carolina, Chapel Hill (1976). An initial interest in the traditional sacred music of southern churches has expanded to include the study of the larger religious systems of which they are a part. A doctoral candidate in anthropology at the University of North Carolina, Chapel Hill, he is engaged in research on American predestinarian Baptists.

CHARLES WILLIAMS received his B.A. in social and political sciences from Rust College in Mississippi in 1969, and holds an M.A. (1976) and a Ph.D. (1981) in anthropology from the University of Illinois at Urbana. His main research interests are in social and political anthropology. He has done field research on black Americans in Mississippi and Tennessee. He is currently teaching at Memphis State University in the Department of Anthropology.

Index

Aesthetics, 5, 80–88
African heritage, 89, 99
African Methodist Episcopal Church, 91, 92
African proverb, 116
African tribal societies, 69, 71, 72, 76
Aging. *See* Older persons
Agricultural Adjustment Act of 1933, 126
Amen corner, 73 (fig. 1)
Anxious seat. *See* Mourners' bench
Appalachia, 26, 27, 30, 32, 146–54; history of, 147–48; isolation of, 147; hillbilly culture, 148; national image of, 149
Appalachian National Forests, 152
Appalachian Regional Commission, 32
Augustine, Saint, 102

Banks, Angeline Hargress, 64 (nn. 15, 17, 26)
Banks, Elijah, 64 (nn. 19, 25, 26)
Baptism, 6, 60, 71, 76, 82, 84–85; description of, 76–78
Baptist church, 78, 92, 140, 143; in Mississippi, 5, 69, 70; diagram of, 73 (fig. 1); doctrine of, 103
Baptist church, Missionary, 5, 80, 81, 91
Baptist church, Primitive, 5, 91, 92, 102–3, 106, 108, 109, 110, 111
Baptists, 72–73, 105, 110, 111, 112, 113, 113 (n. 1)
Basket-making, 18–19
Behavior, 29, 46, 61, 81, 83, 85, 98; and ideology, 3
Bennehan-Cameron black families, 63 (n. 1)
Bessemer, Ala., 62
Bible, 78, 102, 108, 110. *See also individual books of Bible for quotations*
Birmingham, Ala., 62
Black religion or religiosity, 5, 70, 89, 92, 95, 97–99, 100, 116
Blue Ridge Mountains, 56
Body (spiritual), 76, 77, 84, 95
Brokers, 37. *See also* Patronage
Burmese Kachin, 25

Cabbil, Robert, 64 (nn. 17, 19)
Calvinism, 103, 111
Cameron, Betty, 59
Cameron, Duncan, 63 (n. 4)
Cameron, Paul, 55, 56, 57, 63 (nn. 2, 5, 7), 64 (nn. 8, 9)
Cameron, Sandy, 57, 58, 59, 63 (nn. 2, 6)
Cannon, James, 64 (n. 22)
Cannon, Lillie Mae, 64 (n. 22)
Cargo cults, Melanesian, 110
Cartesian dualism, 112
Center for the Study of Historical Preservation, 63 (n. 1)
Charleston, S.C., 13, 19, 22
Charleston Hospital Strike of 1969, 22
Children, 61; tasks of, 13; child-care arrangements, 20; child raising, 27; raising up, 34, 35; filiation, 34, 36; socialization, 73
Christian tenets, 99–100. *See also* Values
Church: spacial arrangements of, 6; membership, 27–28, 89, 92, 103, 112; appearance of, 60, 140, 143; offices, 70; voting in, 70, 76, 78, 83; monetary collections, 74, 78; congregation, 76, 95; community, 80, 90, 111, 140; architecture, 81; exterior v. interior, 82; circuit, 82, 140; rural isolation, 91–92; holiness, 92; visiting other churches, 92; as temple of God, 95; Native American, 117. *See also* Aesthetics, Baptist church, Baptists, Services
Civil War, post–, 146, 147
Class structure: stratification, 5, 6, 36, 37, 38, 131; political and economic powerlessness, 21; middle-class blacks, 46; of farmers, 127, 133, 136–37
Collins, George P., 63 (n. 7)
Colored Primitive Baptist Church, Midway, Fla., 91
Columbus, Mo., 69
Communities, 11, 47, 57, 59, 115, 147; family compounds, 11; activities in, 11–12, 60; post-plantation population, 55–63; Christian, 60; religion, 60; in Appalachia, 146;

identity, 146. *See also* Church, Community
Conversion, 84, 111; experience, 4, 76, 104, 116; ritual, 69–78, 116; major steps in, 71
Cooper River, 11
Courts in North Carolina, 139
Credit, 45, 46, 123, 133, 136. *See also* Debt
Crops: food, 13, 14; cotton, 13, 14, 56, 57, 90, 136; monocrops, 121; animals as, 122, 128, 146; in France, 122; old people as, 125; alternatives to tobacco, 129. *See also* Farms and farming, Tobacco

Dance, religious, 6
Davis, Carrie Hargress, 56, 63 (n. 3), 64 (nn. 19, 23)
Deacons, 74, 76, 77; deacon corner, 73 (fig. 1)
Debt, 13, 16, 62, 123, 124, 128, 141
Depression, the Great, 62, 128
Detroit, Mich., 62
Developers. *See* Industry
Devil, 89, 96–99
Diet, 12, 141
Dirt-affirming and dirt-rejecting views, 98
Disenfranchisement, 4, 135
Dorothy (mother of Ned Forrest Hargress), 59
Dougherty, Molly, 3–4
Duke University Hospital, 139

Economics: inequalities of wealth, 4, 32, 36, 131; marginality, 7; peasant *vis-à-vis* plantation, 11; kinship, 12, 149; industrial, 14; poverty, 31, 37, 89, 91, 131, 136, 149, 151–52, 153; competitive economy, 36; housing prices, 41; gardens, 89, 141, 149; pensions and retirement premiums, 122–25; loans, 123, 133, 136, 141; cash-based economy, 137; labor-intensive v. capital intensive, 137; agricultural, 144; single industry domination of, 146–47; boom-and-bust cycles, 147, 148. *See also* Credit; Debt; Employment, wages; Exchange; Farms and farming, supplemental income, investments; Government agencies and programs, government assistance programs, AFDC; Income; Land, as asset, property taxes, price and value, speculation
Education, 20–21, 148; school integration, 42, 43, 138, 141, 143; rural v. town, 43; reading, 138, 142; for tenant farmers, 138, 142, 143; revenues for, 148, 149
Emancipation, 12, 57, 61, 90, 131
Employment, 41, 61; seasonal, 7, 152; for wages, 7, 11, 13, 18, 90, 91, 129, 144, 146,

147; skilled jobs, 13, 16; gaining, 17; job security, 17; men's, 17–18; women's, 18–20; in hospitals, 19–20; kinship's effect on, 27; access to, 31; possibilities for, 31, 141; in mills, 41, 141; on farms, 41, 142, 144; as domestic workers, 43; urban, 43, 45; as migrant workers, 90, 127; industrial, 129; public work, 142, 146, 153. *See also* Industry
Ecstatic-possession states, 73, 92, 95, 111
Ethnic boundaries, 4, 25–26, 30, 36, 38, 39 (n. 2), 43, 52
Exchange, 44, 45, 46, 125, 136. *See also* Kin networks, Patronage

Family. *See* Kinship
Family compounds, 11, 15, 16
Fanin County, Ga., 152
Farmers Home Administration (FmHA), 42, 47, 141
Farms and farming: crop failure, 6, 7; family farms, 6, 7, 12, 121, 122, 124, 125, 126, 128, 129, 143, 144, 150, 152, 153; French agriculture, 6, 121–25, 128; peasant, 11, 22, 129; displacement of farmers, 11, 122, 134, 141, 143, 144, 150; truck farming, 14; supplemental income, 41, 59, 60, 125, 129, 134, 142, 146, 147, 152–53; corporate farms, 121, 122, 126, 129, 144; management of farm (succession to), 122, 123, 124; investment, 123, 124, 126, 128, 137, 141; categories of farms and farmers, 127; interdependence of farmers, 127; retirement, 127–28; part-time farmers, 127, 129; types of farm sales, 128; competition for land, 128; truck farming, 129; growers' cooperatives, 129; farmers' market, 129; young people leaving farms, 143; changing system of farming, 144; cash crops, 146, 147, 149; subsistence farming, 146, 149; viability of agriculture, 147, 150, 153. *See also* Crops, Tenant farming, Tobacco
Fieldwork or ethnographic methods, 38, 88, 116, 117; autobiographical informant, 5, 69, 78; cross-cultural ethnography, 107
Florida, north, 89
Food stamps, 138, 153
Footwashing, 6
France, 121–25, 128
Franklin County, N.C., 131–44
Franklinton, N.C., 143
Freewill theology, 111
Friendships, 29–30
Function: v. aesthetics, 80; and form, 107

Gatekeepers, 37

General Agricultural census of 1970 (France), 122
Genesis, Book of, 97
Getting religion, 69, 71, 73, 75, 76, 77, 93, 94, 95; confessing religion, 60; being born again, 69, 93, 94, 94–95; joining the church, 69, 110; coming forward, 82, 84; being right on with God, 94, 95; claiming the New Birth, 111; to get saved, 112
Ghost dance, Native American, 110
God, 84, 97, 102, 103, 108, 110, 112, 113; concept of God and Devil, 89, 97–99; knowing God, 93; white Southerner's concept of, 98
Government agencies and programs, 50, 52, 144; government assistance, programs, 7, 138, 143, 152, 153; community action (federal), 42; black v. white agencies, 42; social service organizations, 42, 49, 51, 52; equal opportunity and affirmative action, 47–48; black appointment to, 49; community development funds, 50; low-interest loans, 137; food stamps, 138, 153; cash-share renters' attitude toward welfare, 142–43; welfare, 144; eligibility requirements for Aid to Families with Dependent Children (AFDC), 153
Grass roots, 37
Great Smoky Mountains National Park, 151
Greensboro, Ala., 59, 63 (n. 2)
Greensboro Watchman, 64 (n. 14)

Habakkuk, Book of, 83
Hale County, Ala., 55, 58, 63 (nn. 2, 6), 64 (nn. 9, 11)
Hargis. *See* Hargress
Hargress, variants of, 63 (n. 4)
Hargress, Alice, 63 (n. 2), 64 (nn. 15, 24, 26)
Hargress, Jim, 56, 57, 63 (nn. 4, 6), 64 (n. 9)
Hargress, Ned Forrest, 56, 59–61, 64 (n. 14)
Hargress, Paul, 56–59, 63 (n. 4), 64 (n. 9)
Hargress, Squire, 57
Hargrove. *See* Hargress
Hillbilly culture, 148
Hogis, York, 63 (n. 4)
Holiness churches, 92
Holiness-sanctified movement, 91
Holy City, the, 108
Holy Spirit, 73, 93, 96, 106, 112
Housing, 133, 141–42, 147

Income: family, 13, 127, 136; and marriage, 36; cash, 90, 146; government subsidies (to farmers), 122; retirement premiums (France), 122–25; pensions (France), 125; tobacco allotments as source of, 127; farm income by race, 131; tenant farming incomes, 132 (table 1), 133 (table 2), 134; landlord's share of, 134. *See also* Farms and farming, supplemental income
Indebtedness. *See* Debt
Industry, 61, 90, 149, 152; development of, 3, 11, 12, 27, 28, 37, 143, 147; economy of, 3, 14; tobacco companies, 6, 129; developers in Appalachia, 26, 146–48, 150, 151, 153; cooperation with developers, 32; mills, 41; mines, 61; mineral development, 147; company towns, 147; use of natural resources, 147, 149, 153; employment of cheap labor, 147, 149, 153; recreational/resort, 147, 150–51, 153; textiles, 147, 151; timber, 147, 152, 153; furniture, 151; exploitation, 153
Ireland, succession and land tenure, 124

Jericho, 108
Jesus Christ, 69, 71, 78, 84, 95, 108
John the Baptist, 78
Jones, A. G., 63 (n. 2)
Jordan, River, 78
Joshua, 108
Judaeo-Christian tradition, 99
Judas, 95

Kane, Stephen, 28
Kentucky, eastern, 25–39, 148
Kin networks, 3, 15, 16, 22, 27, 92, 146, 149; exchange, 15, 16, 20, 57–58, 125; to acquire skills, 16, 19–20, 21; to acquire jobs, 17, 27; to educate children, 20–21; financial assistance, 20–21, 133; reciprocity, 31; nuclear family self-reliance, 150
Kinship, 3–4, 15–17, 21, 22, 26, 27, 33, 34, 35, 36, 37, 38, 43, 125, 140, 146; linking communities, 11, 146; and activities, 12, 18, 27; division of labor, 13, 14, 18, 91; entrepreneurial activities, 13, 16, 18; patrilineal descent group, 15; bilateral kindreds, 15; lineage membership, 15; and land, 15, 16, 58, 150; residence, 15, 27, 149; definition of family, 23 (n. 2); groups, 25; as instruments of policy, 25, 147; endogamous demes, 27; exogamous moieties, 27; cousin marriage, 27; patrilineages, 27; ambilineal ramages, 27; communities, 27, 28, 60, 147; sets, 27, 28, 30, 31, 32, 36; householding, 27, 33, 36, 38, 149; loyalties, 28; ideology, 28; generation, 28; collectivities, 28; affines, 29; collaterals, 29; genealogies, 30; disavowal of, 32, 35; dependency training, 34; filiation, 34, 36; adoption, 58;

support, 133; mountain family, 149. *See also* Kin networks

Ku Klux Klan, 53 (n. 4), 140–41; allegory of cat and rats, 140

Labor movements, 23 (n.)

Land: ownership in Appalachia, 7, 33, 146, 147, 150–54; landowning peasantry in Sea Islands, 11; acquisition of, 12, 16, 26, 56, 57, 59, 90, 126, 137, 147, 150; division of, 14, 16, 58; rights to, 15, 16, 57, 153; as asset, 16; policy on, 23 (n. 3); property taxes, 41, 147, 150–51, 152, 153; leasing, 43, 53 (n. 3), 127; and religion, 56; farm labor, 57, 122, 124, 126, 128, 129; for church and school in black post–Civil War community, 57; homesteading, 90; restructuring of landholdings in France, 122, 123, 124; restructuring of landholdings in USA, 136, 150–51; price and value of, 126, 147, 150–51, 153; farm sales, 128; liens and forfeitures, 136; bond between farmer and, 142; speculation, 147, 150, 151; family rooted in, 150, 153; lack of, 151; federal landownership, 151–52; alienation from via public assistance programs, 153. *See also* Land tenure

Land tenure, 6, 7, 90, 127; patterns, 91; and church membership, 92; farm management, 122, 123; succession, 122, 124, 126, 150; tobacco allotments and price of land, 126, 127, 128; farm ownership by nonfarmers, 126, 128; landownership and tenant farming, 137

Last Supper, the, 95

Legislation: civil rights, 22, 52; state and federal enactments, 47, 51; agricultural legislation in France (1960, 1962), 122; on tobacco, 126; legislative control of funds for Appalachia, 147. *See also* Government agencies and programs, Policy, Politics

Lining out hymns, 6

Literature, 107, 108, 115

Little Prairie Creek of Alabama, 60

Lobbying, 6, 128

Louisburg, N.C., 143, 145 (n. 2)

Lowndes County, Miss., 70

Lyles, James, 62, 64 (nn. 27, 28)

McDaniel, George, 63 (n. 1)

Macon County, N.C., 151

Madison County, N.C., 151

Margin (in initiation ritual), 69

Mark, Book of, 78

Marriage, 15, 16, 36, 37, 124, 142, 149; intermarriage, 25; cousin marriage, 27;

endogamous, 43; and church membership, 92; divorce, 142; elopement, 149

Mechanization in agriculture, 121–22, 124, 125, 126, 127, 128, 137

Men, 15, 16–18, 125

Midway, Fla., 89–93, 98

Migration, 4, 14, 30, 61, 91; to North, 15, 19, 133, 140; to acquire skills, 19; forced migration of slaves, 55, 56; out-migration, 56, 91, 148, 152; return migration, 62

Miles, Emma B., 26

Mind, 84, 95

Miracles, 106

Mobility, 30, 37, 90, 131, 147, 153; white mobility and black stability, 131; black mobility as tenant farmers, 134–35, 138–39

Mt. Pleasant, S.C., 11–23

Mt. Zion Baptist Church, Franklin County, N.C., 143

Mourners' bench, 60, 70, 71, 72, 73 (fig. 1), 74–75, 76

Music, style of, 6; singing, 60, 74, 99; church choir, 70; choral, 83; as aesthetic form, 83; music director, 83; camp-meeting or pentecostal, 83; hymn of invitation, 84

Myths, 99, 109–11

Names, 15, 28, 35, 36, 56, 63 (n. 4)

Narratives, 116; oral and personal, 5, 6, 102, 103–4, 105, 106, 110, 111; written, 102, 104–5; as subjective emotional states, 104; oral v. written, 105–6; poetic craft of, 107; symbolic elements of, 107–8; structural patterns of, 108–9; sacred reality, 109, 110; and myths, 109–11; vision/action and myth/ritual, 110. *See also* Testimonies

Native anthropology. *See* Fieldwork or ethnographic methods, autobiographical informant

Natural resources, 147, 148. *See also* Industry, natural resource

New York City, 19–20, 62

North Carolina: western, 30; northeastern fishing community, 80, 81; Outer Banks, 82; Piedmont region, 121, 125–29

North Side Baptist Church, Columbus, Miss., 69, 71

O'Berry, Wilson, 57, 63 (nn. 5, 6, 7), 64 (n. 8)

Old Testament, prophets of, 110

Older persons, 16; the Old People, 12; as farmers, 122, 125, 126; pension (France), 122, 125; pre-retirement and retirement premiums (France), 122–25, 130 (n. 1); policy, 125; reward and gifts, 125; rural

aging in North Carolina, 125–28, 137, 150; retirement of farmers, 126; and land, 150
Oral tradition, religious, 109
Orangeburg, S.C., 21
Ostracism, 71–72

Pakot of Kenya, 86
Paternalism, 38, 43, 44, 47, 100
Patronage, 4, 41, 46; to acquire jobs, 17; white patrons and black brokers, 41, 45, 46, 47, 48, 49, 50, 53, 59; black entrepreneurs, 41, 49, 50–53; intermediaries, 46, 47, 48; younger brokers, 47; and racial violence, 48; brokers' service in civic organizations, 49; brokers and entrepreneurs, 50–53, 53 (n. 1); resources to black organizations, 51. *See also* Exchange
Plantations, 11, 12, 13, 17; owned by Paul Cameron, 55, 56, 57, 60, 62, 63 (n. 1)
Policy, 6, 126, 128; measures, 6; public, 7, 147, 149, 153, 154; urban, 7, 154; desegregation, 20; on land, 23 (n. 3); 147; kinship structures as instruments of, 25; agricultural, 121, 122, 128; pension, 125; tobacco, 125; in culture of poverty model, 148–149; taxation and federal landownership, 151–52; public assistance, 153. *See also* Legislation
Politics, 25, 30, 32, 36, 41, 49, 50, 52; and kinship, 27; elections, 30, 42; elected or appointed political positions, 37, 47, 135; courthouse gang, 42; political instability (post–Civil War), 57; of tobacco, 125, 126, 128, 129; tobacco lobby, 128
Poverty. *See* Economics, poverty
Praise House, 12
Prayer, 6, 74, 94, 99, 106
Preaching: ecstatic, 6, 74; oratory, 6, 83, 106; role of preacher, 74, 75, 77, 95, 106; hiring and firing of preacher, 82, 83
Predestinarian theology, 111, 112
Protestants, 98, 99, 111
Puritans, 102, 106

Quakers, 102

Race relations, 43, 47, 89, 127, 131; white domination, 13, 14, 16, 21, 23, 43, 49, 59, 97; desegregation policies, 20; civil rights legislation, 22, 52; discrimination, 22; integration, 42, 48; segregation, 42, 43, 99, 138; white and black economic relationship, 43, 44, 45; contractual arrangements, 44; reputation of whites, 44, 45; social aspects, 44–45; exchange between races, 44, 46; reputation of blacks, 46; attitudes, 46;

potential violence, 48; rape incident, 59; racial identity, 59, 100; racism, 89, 91, 98, 100, 143; religious inferiority, 100; in tenant farming, 132, 136, 138, 139, 142–43; attitudes v. actions, 140. *See also* Patronage
Rainey, Louis, 63 (n. 3), 64 (nn. 10, 12, 13, 15, 16, 18, 20, 22, 26)
Reaggregation (in initial ritual), 69
Reformation, the, 102
Regional identity, Southern, 116
Research methods. *See* Fieldwork and ethnographic methods
Residence patterns, 29, 30, 43, 45. *See also* Settlement patterns
Revelation, Book of, 108
Revivals, 60, 69, 72, 75, 76, 111; scheduling of, 70; motivation for, 70; activities during, 74
Right hand of the fellowship, 71, 78
Rite of passage, 69, 85
Ritual, 110, 116
Roberts, Oral, 102
Roman Catholic Church, 106

Sacks, Karen, 23
Scriptures, 74, 77, 108, 110
Sea Island community. *See* Mt. Pleasant, S.C.
Segmentation, 29, 30, 32
Senate and House Agricultural Committees, 130 (n. 3)
Separation (in initiation ritual), 69, 108
Sermons, 74, 92, 95, 99, 106
Service (religious), 92, 96; orders of, 6; devotional, 74; functions of, 82–83; call to worship, 83; aesthetic aspects of, 84; hymn of invitation, 84; communion, 95
Settlement pattern, 26, 91. *See also* Land, Residence patterns
Sharecropping. *See* Tenant farming, sharecropping
Shouting, 6, 95
Simpkins, Karen Li, 27
Sinners, 70, 71, 72
Sinners' seat. *See* Mourners' bench
Slavery, 4, 12, 43, 47, 55, 57, 60, 69, 89, 99; slave register (1844), 55; churches established during, 90; slave religion, 99
Smell as aesthetic form, 86–87
Soul, 84
South, antebellum, 69
Southern Anthropological Society, vii
Southern Historical Collection (SHC), University of North Carolina, 63 (nn. 2, 6, 7), 64 (n. 8)
Southern studies, 116

Stack, Carol B., 130
Stagville Plantation in North Carolina, 63
    (n. 1)
Subsistence agriculture. *See* Farms and farm-
    ing, subsistence farming
Swain County, N.C., 151–52

Taxation. *See* Land, Policy
Tenant farming, 6–7, 43, 126, 131–45; cash-
    tenancy, 6, 132, 133, 134 (table 3), 136,
    141–43, 144; cash-share farming, 6, 132,
    133, 134, 135 (table 3), 136, 144; share-
    cropping, 7, 44, 53 (n. 3), 90, 131, 132,
    133, 134, 135, 137–41; types of, 131–37;
    black v. white, 132, 135; income from,
    133–34; relationship with landlord, 134,
    135, 136, 137, 139, 141, 144; population
    (distribution), 136, 144; economics of,
    136–37, 141; risk, 137; description of
    sharecroppers, 137, 144; cash-tenant's atti-
    tude toward, 142
Testimonies, 6, 73, 75, 102, 106; acceptance
    of Christ, 71, 75–76; spiritual experience,
    94; bearing witness, 95. *See also* Narra-
    tives, Visionary experiences
Tobacco, 90, 136, 146, 149; companies, 6,
    129; history and economics of, 130 (n. 3);
    antismoking campaigns, 129; yield, 133;
    price and profit, 133–34; average acreages
    worked, by class, 135 (table 3); burley,
    146, 149
Tobacco allotments, 6, 7, 43–44, 126–28,
    135; distribution of, 126; as a resource,
    126, 127; leasing of, 126–27; average size
    of, 127
Toning the bell, 60
Trickster figure, 99

Unions, 20, 22, 42, 47, 153
United States Department of Agriculture, 43,
    53 (n. 3), 133, 145 (n. 2)

United States Forest Service, 151; as land-
    owner, 152

Values (ethical), 61, 149; communal, 3; repu-
    tation, 35, 37, 44, 45, 46; security and
    independence, 58; Christian, 61; stressed in
    sermons, 92; departure from and the Devil,
    96–97; white, 98; public speaking, 106; of
    cash-tenant farmers, 143
Visionary experiences, 94, 103–16 passim;
    and dream states, 93, 110; as oral litera-
    ture, 107, 108; akin to myths, 109–11, 112
Voting, 27, 42, 138, 143; disenfranchisement,
    4, 135; voter registration drives, 42, 64
    (n. 14); voter education programs, 50; in
    church, 70, 76, 78

Wallace, Joel, 64 (nn. 22, 23)
Washington, Betty Hargress, 64 (nn. 13, 15,
    18)
Wautauga County, N.C. 150, 152
Weeks Act (1911), 152
Welfare, 31, 32, 38
Wesley (squad leader, Alabama plantation),
    63 (n. 6)
West Virginia, 62
Williams, Minnie Hargress, 64 (n. 17)
Willingness to be saved (conversion ritual),
    71–72
Winthrop, John, 102
Women, 18–20, 124; as farmers, 14, 20, 91,
    137, 142, 152; wage alternatives, 18; wage
    employment, 18, 19–20; financial indepen-
    dence, 20; role in resistance movements,
    22; French retirement premium, 122; old,
    125

YMCA, 104
Young adults, 121, 123, 124, 143, 144